Eureka!

the science and art of insights

Andrew Grenville

2020

ISBN 9781658613255

Book design by Emineh Babayan
Cover design by Wysp Creative
Author photo by John Weight Photography

Maru Group
Toronto, Canada

www.marugroup.net

Table of contents

Chapter 1: The curious nature of insights

"Imagination is more important than knowledge. For knowledge is limited, whereas imagination embraces the entire world, stimulating progress, giving birth to evolution."
Albert Einstein

Insights are elusive creatures. They don't come when called. They won't follow deadlines. And they refuse to respect traditions. But they do upend the world, and they delight us when everything clicks into place and, suddenly, we understand. Eureka!

Insights come from acting like magpies, picking up new ideas and pieces of information as if they were shiny objects you can't resist—and then seeking connections between them. Insights come from ignoring boundaries, making analogies, and going for walks. This book is about all those things.

Insights about insights come from unusual places; spies, doctors, inventors, detectives, psychologists, writers, and musicians all have experiences and ideas that can inform insights professionals. We'll hear from all of them.

This story about weaving together insights begins with the tale of a Frenchman born in 1742.

Looming insights

Joseph Marie Jacquard was from Lyon, at the confluence of the Rhône and Saône rivers. He never went to school and was illiterate until age 13, when his brother-in-law took him under his wing. Over the course of his life, Jacquard made straw hats, sold real estate, bound books, manufactured cutlery, made printing type, processed lime for mortar, and fought in the French revolutionary army. He tried weaving too, because it had been his father's trade. But he found that too difficult and quit.

By midlife he was bankrupt and forced to live off his wife's savings. It wasn't until he was almost 50 that he unpromisingly began to tinker with machinery. His greatest invention links the computer I am writing on, the Luddite uprising during the Industrial Revolution and the sweater I am wearing. Jacquard's story epitomizes the process of generating ideas, insights and innovations. It is not the story of a lone genius. It is an account of incremental insight, making connections, and crossing boundaries.

His invention, the Jacquard loom, revolutionized the weaving industry. It enabled mass production and allowed for finer and more flexible designs, produced more economically than had been possible before. His big insight was that punch cards could be used efficiently to automate the loom in better, faster ways.

Jacquard's economical employment of punch cards inspired the English inventor Charles Babbage to utilize them in his analytical engine, which was the first design of a general-purpose computer. Then Herman Hollerith extended the use of punch cards to record and store information for the 1890 US census, enabling large scale data crunching at speed. Hollerith later formed the company we know as IBM. Sometimes an insight can have a long reverberation.

Into the deep

An insight is "a clear, deep, and sometimes sudden understanding," according to the Cambridge Dictionary. But insights don't materialize on their own. There is a process. And an insight can't come from just one source. It comes from combining multiple pieces of information in unique ways, building on what has been learned before. That often involves drawing on learnings from other fields, either directly or by analogy.

Generating an insight involves five steps: gathering raw materials, working them over in your mind, letting your unconscious mind seek out new and different connections, having a eureka moment when the idea surfaces, and having the insight validated.

In this way, an insight differs from an observation or a research finding. They are stand-alone pieces of information; an insight is connected, never isolated. Insights also differ from the product of analytic thought, which uses deliberate, step-by-step procedures.

An insight is a wilder beast. It's a leap forward, unpredictable and untameable.

You can create the conditions for good insights, and you can avoid traps which derail or limit them, but you can't beckon an insight and reliably command it to sit up or play fetch. You can't do that with my dog either, but she comes into the story later.

Fractal thought

Insights are identical in structure to ideas, innovations, and scientific paradigm shifts. They are the same shape, but of a different scale. They follow a fractal pattern. Whether you zoom in or zoom out, the form is the same.

Ideas come from what we know and what we absorb. We mull things over and look for new connections. Our unconscious mind churns away and then, at a time of its own choosing, an idea occurs to us. Then we try it out. The same is true for innovation, as we'll see in the story of Jacquard. Paradigm shifts in science occur when bright ideas lead to insight, to innovation, and ultimately to an accumulation of fresh understandings that force us to rethink our view of the world. The pattern is the same in each case.

The graphic on this page is a simple example of a fractal pattern. In this case, it is a Koch fractal. It is based on the Koch curve, named after Swedish mathematician Helge von Koch.

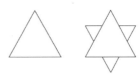

Fractal patterns occur beautifully throughout nature. Consider the glory of snowflakes, nautilus shells, ferns, the fjords of Norway, and the stunning logarithmic spiral of a Romanesco

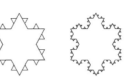

broccoli. It's no surprise fractals occur in our thought and culture too, but it is exciting. And that's the thing.

Insights are exhilarating. Moments of insight are why most of us get up in the morning. Sure, within our organizations, the insights departments are not generally seen as the pinnacle of excitement. But we know the thrill of the hunt and the excited anticipation of waiting for an insight to burst forth from the shadows with a resounding aha!

Weaving a tale

Jacquard's invention has an unlikely origin. It involves a newspaper from England, the French Revolution, a net, and Napoleon Bonaparte. But it has many of the classic features of ideas, insights, and innovations.

Steven Johnson, in his book *Where Good Ideas Come From*, observes, "We have a natural tendency to romanticize breakthrough innovations, imagining momentous ideas transcending their surroundings, a gifted mind somehow seeing over the detritus of old ideas and ossified tradition. But ideas are works of bricolage; they are built out of that detritus. We take the ideas that we've inherited or that we've stumbled across and rejigger them into some new shape."

Jacquard rejiggered the work of previous loom makers. The evolution began in 1725 with Basile Bouchon, the son of an organ maker and a weaver. Automated organs played their music using rotating pegged cylinders. Bouchon observed that the information inscribed onto these cylinders was first laid out on paper. His aha moment came when he realized perforated paper could code information about patterns, and that he could use punched paper to encode weaving patterns for the loom. He made connections across disciplines and, boom: an insight.

His invention used a broad strip of punched paper to select the warp threads that would be raised during weaving. In innovatively combining organs and looms, Bouchon displayed a cross-disciplinary pattern that we'll observe over and over as we explore insights.

Jacques Vaucanson extended Bouchon's ideas to create the first automated loom. He was an expert in automata—which were all the rage in the 1700's European high society. Automata were typically mechanical recreations of people and animals. Vaucanson, for example, created an automaton that looked and moved like a man and could play the flute. He created another that was a life-sized duck with 400 moving parts that could swim, quack, flap its wings, drink water, eat, and seemingly excrete. In the course of creating this odd duck he invented the first known flexible rubber tube, so that he could create the duck's intestines. His insight in loom-making was to take Bouchon's idea and add to it his knowledge of automation. Again, we see the combination of cross-disciplinary ideas creating something unique.

Maria Popova writes a wonderful blog called Brain Pickings, which celebrates insight and creativity. In her mission statement she says, "I believe that creativity is a combinatorial force—it happens when existing pieces of knowledge, ideas, memories and inspiration coalesce into incredible new formations. And in order to make a concept (or product, or idea, or argument) fully congeal in your head, you have to first understand all the little pieces that surround it—pieces across art, design, music, science, technology, philosophy, cultural history, politics, psychology, sociology, ecology, anthropology, you-name-itology. Pieces that build your mental pool of resources, which you then combine into original concepts that are stronger, smarter, richer, deeper and more impactful—the foundation of creativity."

6 / Eureka! The science and art of insights

Cast your net

Jacquard built on the ideas of Bouchon and Vaucanson by also drawing on his own varied background. But why he did so is intriguing. In his 1878 book *The History and Principles of Weaving - By Hand and by Power,* Alfred Barlow recounts Sir John Bowering's testimony in front of a committee of the UK House of Commons about the origins of the Jacquard loom. Sir Bowering had visited Jacquard in France after his invention had become popular.

Jacquard, who was broke at the time he created his invention, was looking for ways to make some cash. That's when he came across a contest that offered a prize. Bowering reports, "his attention had never been turned to mechanical topics till the Peace of Amiens opened the communication of France with England; at the same time an extract from an English newspaper fell into his hands, in which it was stated that a society here offered a premium to any man who should weave a net by machinery."

Drawing on his prior experience making straw hats, Jacquard thought he could invent such a machine, and, indeed, he did. He gave one of the nets he produced to a friend and, as Bowering recounts, "The net by some means or other got into the hands of the authorities and was sent to Paris." He was soon summoned by the local governor who declared, "I require you to make the machine which led to this result." Jacquard built one, as ordered, and it was sent to Paris.

Suddenly, an order came for his arrest, and Jacquard was unceremoniously and abruptly bundled off to Paris under the guard of a gendarme. He was taken to "the Conservatory of Arts, to produce the machine in the presence of inspectors." Bowering explains the arrest: "It was in Bonaparte's time, when things were done in a rash and very arbitrary way." At the meeting at the Conservatory of Arts, Jacquard was interrogated by Napoleon Bonaparte himself.

"He was introduced to Bonaparte…who said to him with a menace of incredulity, 'Are you the man who pretends to do that which God Almighty cannot do, to tie a knot in a stretched string?' He produced the machine, and officials, satisfied that Jacquard's net-making invention worked, took him to see a loom "on which twenty or thirty thousand francs had been expended for the production of articles for the use of Bonaparte." Bowering says, "He offered to do that by a simple machine which they were attempting to do by a very complicated one...." And thus, he set about inventing the Jacquard loom.

He developed the ideas of Vaucanson, who built on those of Bouchon and many others. But his insight made for a more reliable and flexible production of unlimited varieties of pattern weaving. Jacquard's exploits echoed the words of Sir Isaac Newton: "If I have seen further, it is by standing on the shoulders of giants."

This famous 17th century quote about how Newton's genius came from building upon previous learnings is, quite fittingly, itself a reworking of earlier ideas. It can be traced back to at least the 12th century, when Isaiah di Trani wrote, "Who sees further, a dwarf or a giant? Surely a giant, for his eyes are situated at a higher level than those of the dwarf. But if the dwarf is placed on the shoulders of the giant, who sees further? .... So too we are dwarfs astride the shoulders of giants. We master their wisdom and move beyond it."

That's how insights work. We build on what is known and make fresh connections between things like wooden quacking ducks that swim and poop, self-playing organs and looms. We weave it all together and create something revolutionary. But Jacquard, Napoleon Bonaparte and the industrialists of England were not quite ready for what this set of insights unleashed.

Upsetting insights

Insights change things. By offering new opportunities, insights can upend the existing order. Some people welcome that. Others feel threatened, because it requires them to change.

The weavers of Lyon were not happy about Jacquard's invention. They felt threatened, because it challenged their traditional way of working. They rioted, smashing and burning one of his looms in the public square. Jacquard was forced to flee Lyon three times because of threats on his life.

In England, angry workers—who belonged to an organization of textile workers called the Luddites—seized on Jacquard looms as symbols of an unwelcome industrial revolution and publicly destroyed some, before setting them alight. Insights can be upsetting. But that doesn't negate their importance.

In the square in Lyon where a loom went up in flames there now stands a monument to Jacquard. Charles Babbage was so impressed with Jacquard's insights he purchased an expensive and elegant portrait of Jacquard that was woven in fine silk on a Jacquard loom. It is so intricate that 24,000 punch cards were required to program it. Babbage hung the portrait in his workshop as an homage. Today it is in the collection of the Science Museum in London. Insights win out in the end.

The insights industry is currently going through its own revolution. What used to be an industry that was reactive and focused on the traditional tools of surveys and focus groups is now faced with an urgent need to proactively absorb the multitude of streams of information now available to us. The advent of big data, social media, automated DIY research, and AI has required, and will continue to require, radical change in the insights industry's business model.

We can either burn big data in the public square, or we can focus on the essential task at hand: generating insights. I say let's pursue the aha moment. That's where the fun is.

About this book

This book is about insights. It starts with looking at how we learn and how we make connections. It then moves on to look at how biases—cognitive and otherwise—can limit our insights or lead us astray. Next it examines strategies that can help us avoid or mitigate those biases. The final portion shines a light on the process of generating insights, exploring ways we can improve and enhance them.

Our industry tends to treat research as an individual sport, but one of the recurring themes in the book is the value of teamwork. As Steven Johnson notes in *Where Good Ideas Come From*, "most great ideas first take shape in a partial, incomplete form. They have the seeds of something profound, but they lack a key element that can turn the hunch into something truly powerful. And more often than not, that missing element is somewhere else, living as another hunch in another person's head."

The insights industry tends to be insular. But the reality is that, when we look up and cast about, there are a whole host of other people who do basically the same thing: they absorb mounds of information—qualitative and quantitative, big and small—and then distill that data into insights. There is great benefit in better understanding how they approach insights.

As physicist Tom McLeish writes in *The Poetry and Music of Science*, "Little of the radically new emerges from a narrow obsession or labour within established boundaries. There is value in broad, 'interdisciplinary' excursion…for the new patterns and connections that they offer for specific creative demands. Although the most distant connections require the deepest and longest incubation, even at the still-mysterious depths of the non-conscious, the long wait for their surfacing is worth the patience."

The other sense-makers we look to include intelligence analysts, doctors, lawyers, detectives, archeologists, historians, sociologists, and psychologists. Throughout the book I draw on interviews with, and the literature of, these fellow sense-makers. The aim is to cross boundaries and make fresh connections.

Chapter 2: Making linkages is the first step in the journey to insight

"Intelligence analysts must understand themselves before they can understand others."
Richards J. Heuer, Jr.

The insights industry is about transforming information into insights. Information is raw material. Insights come from distilling that information and then putting it in context by making connections to other knowledge.

As we journey from information to insights, we must navigate the maze of our minds. By better understanding how our minds work, we can realize when we've gone down a blind alley and course correct, and when we should proceed full speed ahead. The journey starts with looking at how we learn, right from the beginning.

Making connections

When we are born, we come equipped with a variety of hardwired abilities. Even though our vision is poor, we pay special attention to faces, and we are quickly able to identify the faces of our mother and other important people. We are automatically attracted to the sound of speech over other sounds and pay closer attention to higher-pitched voices (hence, baby talk). When something brushes a baby's cheek, they turn to it, and when something is put in their mouth, they suck.

Then we start learning. Bit by bit, we start making connections, layering one piece of information on top of the previous one. When we put together that the special face and breast brushing against our face equals dinner, we start the ball rolling. When we realize that the thing that is poking us in the eye is our own hand, and that we can stop it from hitting ourselves, we're picking up momentum.

We learn by linking new information to what we already know. And that process never stops. We are continually making connections between what we have seen before and what we are seeing for the first time. These connections have important implications for how we come to an insight, because they are the only route to fresh thinking.

We cannot leap from point A to point C without first connecting to point B. This process of making connections provides both amazing opportunities and potential problems.

The roots of learning

This process of making connections is how all living creatures learn and navigate their lives. Humans have been the most successful at making connections, allowing us to make incredible advances in science and art. Both innovation and creativity spring from this ability to make new and unique connections. Formally, this process is referred to as apperception.

In psychology, apperception is "the process by which new experience is assimilated to and transformed by the residuum of past experience of an individual to form a new whole." Pioneering psychologist and philosopher William James writes in his 1899 book *Talks to Teachers on Psychology*, "In all the apperceptive operations of the mind, a certain general law makes itself felt—the law of economy. In admitting a new body of experience, we instinctively seek to disturb as little as possible our pre-existing stock of ideas." This points to the strength and weakness of how we learn.

The strength is that we can expand our base of knowledge by seeing patterns and similarities and connecting the new information with the old. The weakness is that it is easy to draw false parallels and therefore arrive at incorrect conclusions.

"I think that you see plainly enough now that the process of apperception is what I called it a moment ago, a resultant of the association of ideas," James writes. "The product is a sort of fusion of the new with the old, in which it is often impossible to distinguish the share of the two factors. For example, when we listen to a person speaking or read a page of print, much of what we think we see or hear is supplied from our memory. We overlook misprints, imagining the right letters, though we see the wrong ones; and how little we actually hear, when we listen to speech, we realize when we go to a foreign theatre; for there what troubles us is not so much that we cannot understand what the actors say as that we cannot hear their words. The fact is that we hear quite as little under similar conditions at home, only our mind, being fuller of English verbal associations, supplies the requisite material for comprehension upon a much slighter auditory hint."

In other words, we fill in the blanks based on what we know already. That way we don't have to think so hard. That's why when you go someplace you have never been before, it always seems to take much longer to get there than to get back. When we are heading someplace new, we have to pay attention and check to make sure we are on the right track. We're processing lots of information to ensure we don't miss anything. On the way back we can go on autopilot because our mind will fill in the gaps.

Great pigs that carry men

This ability to fill in the blanks allows us to make rapid links, even in the face of missing information. But how well we make those connections influences how well we understand the new material. James continues, "We always try to name a new experience in some way which will assimilate it to what we already know. We [struggle with] anything absolutely new, anything without any name, and for which a new name must be forged. So we take the nearest name, even though it be inappropriate. A child will call snow, when he sees it for the first time, sugar or white butterflies. The sail of a boat he calls a curtain; an egg in its shell, seen for the first time, he calls a pretty potato; an orange, a ball; a folding corkscrew, a pair of bad scissors. Caspar Hauser called the first geese he saw horses, and the Polynesians called Captain Cook's horses pigs. Mr. Rooper has written a little book on apperception, to which he gives the title of "*A Pot of Green Feathers*," that being the name applied to a pot of ferns by a child who had never seen ferns before."

Our understanding of something obviously ripens as we make additional connections. While it made sense to Polynesians seeing horses for the first time to call them "great pigs that carry men," and goats "birds with great teeth in their heads," they soon developed a more nuanced understanding of these animals.

This ability to fill in the blanks opens the door to learning through analogies. This not only allows us to make creative leaps, but also enables us to make imprecise connections that permit us to grasp things that, at first, are difficult to understand.

Rome is like Philly

Questlove is the drummer for the hip-hop band the Roots, a DJ, an actor, a writer, and an all-round creative type. In his book *Creative Quest* he writes about how we learn, create, and communicate by linking something new to something we know. "We have metaphors because people's minds try to make two unalike things like each other," he says. "We have creativity largely because of metaphors."

He illustrates this with a story. "I know a woman who grew up with me in Philadelphia. She went to Rome when we were in our early twenties, and when she came back, she told me about it. Her description was good and detailed, but it was also based on Philly. This plaza reminded her of Rittenhouse Square, a little. There was a building that had some of the same feel as the Academy of Music. It wasn't just that she had limited context, though that was part of it. It wasn't just that she was talking to me, who also had limited context, though that was part of it. It was new ideas growing out of old ones."

About an acre

Can you picture how big an acre of land is? I can look it up and learn an acre is 43,560 square feet, but that doesn't help me. I know that Toronto's High Park, just two blocks from my house, is 400 acres.

Having spent many hours walking the dog through its trails in the woods, across soccer pitches, and through formal gardens, I know it is large, diverse, and very beautiful. But I can't mentally subdivide it by 400 and have that make any real tangible sense to me. I can't quite get my head around it.

Richard Saul Wurman, perhaps best known as one of the founders of TED talks, wrote a book called *Information Anxiety*. I read it years ago, and in it he provides a description of how big an acre is. He uses that description as an illustration of how we can make something understandable by connecting it to something we already know.

"An acre is basically the same size as a football field without the endzones," he writes. Now can you picture how big an acre is?

That parallel has stuck with me over the years because it's a brilliant example of how we learn by making connections, even if the connections are approximate. A football field is actually a little bigger than an acre, but that's okay. It's close enough that I can make a connection between the two. This connection of the two allows me to take something that I can't really get my head around and transform it into something I can picture and relate to.

Don't pet the big cat

The ability to learn by drawing parallels cuts both ways, though. It is very easy for us to draw connections that lead us to faulty understandings. Let's say, for example, that I am a cat owner, and my cat is a very friendly orange tabby that loves to have her belly rubbed. And let's say that I don't know what a tiger is, and I find myself strolling through a steaming jungle in Tamil Nadu, India. Imagine I encounter a very large cat that reminds me of my tabby at home. I am going to be in trouble if I think, "Hey, my cat is friendly and loves to get her belly rubbed, I bet this big cat will too." My mistake is to assume too close a connection, too much similarity.

This kind of false analogy can blind us to differences between markets or lead us to assume needs that don't exist. We need to be careful when we draw analogies and make connections. It's a jungle out there.

One foot in front of the other

Learning by making linkages is the first step in the journey to insights. Our brain is the vehicle that takes us from input to insight. To make the journey we need to know how that vehicle works, what its quirks are, and how we can correct for them, or at least recognize and grapple with them.

As we travel along, we need to recognize that what we know now may not be the complete picture, or even a good representation of reality. Insights depend on the connections we make.

Chapter 3: Easy connections can misdirect

"We see only what we know."
Johann Wolfgang von Goethe

The journey to insights has more twists and turns, peaks and valleys, deserts to cross and streams to ford than we generally acknowledge. There is more that is unknown than we care to admit. Mysteries abound, and sometimes we are blind to them because we think we know the answer. We interpret new information by making connections to what we already believe. When we make those associations it feels right, and we assume we have a good understanding—even when we might be off the mark.

"That makes sense." That's what we say when presented with a new piece of information that we can readily slot into our pre-existing knowledge. It is like having a piece of a puzzle snap into place. It feels right, and it reinforces what we already believe.

Conversely, a new piece of information that does not seem to fit is challenging. Do we disregard it as aberrant? Or is it the key to unlocking a new understanding?

Sticking to our guns

We pay more attention to information that supports the way we see the world. And we are more likely to reject information that contradicts what we currently believe. This tendency to ignore information that does not fit with what we expect has been observed in many settings, but it is particularly well studied in the field of politics. For example, one meta-analysis of 51 studies on this phenomenon found "both liberal and conservative participants showed a robust tendency to find otherwise identical information more valid and compelling when it confirmed rather than challenged their political affinities." In other words, we tend to dismiss information we don't want to hear.

The problem is that this tendency to stick with what makes sense or confirms our pre-existing beliefs can hold us back from a more complete understanding. And what we don't know can hurt us.

History reveals how paying attention to information that seems to make sense, and ignoring or misinterpreting information that does not seem to fit, can have devastating consequences; it has led people to inadvertently maim and kill and has delayed breakthroughs that can change the world. But when we pay close attention to data that doesn't currently make sense, we can spark a fresh insight that changes everything.

Humor me

From the time of Ancient Greece to well into the 1800s, European physicians were certain that the body was governed by four humors—fluids that determined our health. Hippocrates, often considered the father of modern medicine, was a popularizer of this theory. In his treatise *On the Nature of Man* he describes it this way: "The Human body contains blood, phlegm, yellow bile and black bile. These are the things that make up its constitution and cause its pains and health. Health is primarily that state in which these constituent substances are in the correct proportion to each other, both in strength and quantity, and are well mixed. Pain occurs when one of the substances presents either a deficiency or an excess or is separated in the body and not mixed with others."

The qualities of the humors were thought to influence the nature of the diseases they caused. Yellow bile, for example, caused warm diseases, and phlegm caused cold diseases. Treatments such as bloodletting, emetics, and purges were aimed at expelling excess amounts of a humor. Herbs were also used. Chamomile, for example, was used to decrease heat and lower excessive bile. And arsenic was used in a poultice bag to 'draw out' the excess humors that led to symptoms of the plague. George Washington died after asking to be bled heavily to treat a throat infection he had.

This thinking dominated medicine for over 2,000 years, even though people repeatedly saw evidence that contradicted this seemingly common-sense explanation. It was clear that the treatments were not effective. But people paid attention to the information that seemed to support the theory and ignored that which contradicted it—to the point that when people died it was seen as a consequence of the disease and not the treatment. That's being blinded by common sense.

For a person whose credo was "first, do no harm," Hippocrates's theories had some very harmful effects.

Los lobos

The year 1874 saw the births of Winston Churchill, Herbert Hoover, Harry Houdini, and António Egas Moniz. Moniz is less well known than the others, but he did grow up to become a celebrated neurologist who was awarded the Nobel Prize for Medicine.

Moniz believed that mental illness originated from abnormal neural connections. He described a "fixation of synapses" which, in mental illness, was expressed as "predominant, obsessive ideas." In 1935, Moniz traveled from his native Portugal to London to attend the Second International Congress of Neurology. There he saw Yale neuroscientist John Fulton and his junior colleague Carlyle Jacobsen present their research on the cortical function of primates. They had brought with them two chimpanzees: Becky and Lucy.

Becky and Lucy were lab animals that were brought along to represent the results of an experimental intervention. Before the experiment, Becky and Lucy tended to get very frustrated if they performed an experimental task poorly and, as a result, did not get a reward. They, especially Becky, would pitch a fit, get agitated, roll around on the floor, scream, defecate, and throw feces at the scientists. Fulton decided they were perfect candidates for testing out a new surgical procedure. He had already learned that cortical lesions could lead to both paralysis and involuntary, jerky muscle movements. And he had determined that a "bilateral frontal lobe ablation" destroyed mental skills.

When he removed Becky and Lucy's frontal lobes, he found that it did indeed devastate their mental abilities. Their performance on tests was greatly diminished. But he noticed other changes as well. The once emotional and aggressive Becky no longer cared if she failed the experimental tasks and did not get a reward. Instead, she was docile and unperturbed. It was suggested that she behaved as if she had joined a "happiness cult."

At the same conference, Henri Claude, a French neuropsychiatrist, hosted a symposium on the function of the frontal lobes, featuring papers by neurologists, neurosurgeons, and psychologists. In that session Claude concluded that "altering the frontal lobes profoundly modifies the personality of subjects."

Moniz was greatly impressed, as both the papers and the result of the experiment with Becky and Lucy fit with his theory that mental illness resulted from abnormal neural connections, and that the frontal lobe played an important role. Within three months Moniz had tried this procedure—which he called a leucotomy—on twenty patients. We know it better today as a lobotomy.

There were complications, which included "increased temperature, vomiting, bladder and bowel incontinence, diarrhea, and ocular affections such as ptosis and nystagmus, as well as psychological effects such as apathy, akinesia, lethargy, timing and local disorientation, kleptomania, and abnormal sensations of hunger." Moniz suggested that these effects were likely only temporary.

He concluded that of these twenty patients, seven improved significantly, seven were somewhat improved, and the remaining six were unchanged. Feeling these results strongly supported his theories, he promoted his findings in journal articles and at lectures. He found a receptive audience in Italy, where almost 200 lobotomies were performed by 1939. Interest in the procedure quickly spread and, in 1949, Moniz was awarded the Nobel Prize for his work on lobotomies.

One factor that increased the popularity of lobotomies was the innovations of American neurologist Walter Jackson Freeman II.

He was seeking to make lobotomies quicker and easier to perform. His ultimate approach allowed him to do lobotomies in an office setting in just minutes. He would knock out his patients using electroshock therapy and hammer an icepick into their brains through their eye sockets, and then sever the connections to the frontal lobes. It was quick and efficient.

It is estimated that over 66,000 people had been lobotomized by the time the procedure fell out of favor in the 1960s. Approximately 5% died during the procedure, and the effects on the others were profound. But it did make some people easier to manage.

Context is king

What happened with lobotomies is an extreme case of what can happen when we filter information through our expectations. It was easy for Moniz to connect what he saw with Becky and Lucy to the ideas and perspectives he already had. He and all the other surgeons who did these lobotomies were not monsters. Nor were the Nobel Prize committee fools. Physicians were (and are) facing a formidable challenge with mental illness, with few therapeutic options.

When I was a teenager, I worked at the Penrose Asylum in the summers. It was a Victorian prison-like structure, built in the mid-1800's, before Canada was a country. It was essentially a dismal warehouse for deeply unusual and difficult-to-control people. The original architect called the rooms for sleeping "cells," and that's certainly what they felt like. In the basement there were still hand and leg cuffs built into the wall, so that patients could be restrained—because, when the asylum was built, there were very few alternatives when people became agitated.

When I worked there, at the dawn of the eighties, almost all the residents were heavily sedated with haloperidol, an anti-psychotic. I noticed that many of them had strange tics—small repetitive motions. Some would flick their tongue in and out, or smack their lips, or grimace, over and over again. Others would rapidly flutter their hands or continuously jerk their head back and forth. Being 16 and naïve, I assumed this was simply a manifestation of their mental illness. But it was not. I later learned it was an irreversible side effect of the high doses of the anti-psychotics they were receiving, which were functioning like chemical restraints. The use of these medications was a late 20th century version of being chained up in the basement or given a lobotomy.

In this context, it's a little easier to see how lobotomies seemed like a good idea at the time. There was an unmet need for therapeutic options. The practice fit with an emerging theory about abnormal neural connections in the frontal lobe. And there was a chimpanzee whose behavior had changed in a way that made her easier to handle.

Moniz looked at the information that made sense to him and inadvertently filtered out the information that did not support his position. It's an all too easy trap to fall into. We do it all the time, and we don't even notice it.

Makes sense

The theory of our health being ruled by the four humors made sense for over 2,000 years. For a few decades, so did the idea of lobotomies. These notions seemed right in the context. But they were not the best ideas. They were the product of common sense, which is defined as "sound practical judgment that is independent of specialized knowledge, training." We need to question what seems to be common sense in our research practices. Sometimes our received wisdom is nonsense. And we must develop the specialized knowledge and training that sheds light on our analytic blind spots.

Chapter 4: The pattern-seeking brain

"Human beings are pattern-seeking animals who will prefer even a bad theory or a conspiracy theory to no theory at all."
Christopher Hitchens

I had the good fortune recently to spend a few days up north, far from the bright lights of the big city. At night the stars lit up the sky, and as I stepped outside my eyes quickly gravitated to familiar patterns like the Big Dipper and Orion's Belt.

As I found myself trying to recall the ancient stories behind these groupings of stars, I was struck by how we naturally seek out and see patterns. Each culture, around the world, has developed stories to explain the patterns people see in the stars. Some of them are similar— mainly because good stories spread—and some are quite different. It's like reading tea leaves. People excel at making up stories and explaining causal links based on the scantest information. That's how fortune tellers, clairvoyants, and psychics stay in business.

We intuitively concoct stories to explain the "patterns" we see—even when the connections are random and spurious. This observation has important implications for the research and insights industry, both for how we interpret research results and how we ask questions.

Our brains work from sparse data and fill in the blanks, making connections that may or may not actually be there. This practice is hardwired into our body and brain and is responsible for our very existence. We do this pattern-seeking instantaneously and without conscious thought.

Make connections or die

In his book *The Believing Brain,* Michael Shermer explains why we are wired to make connections that may or may not be there: "Imagine you are a hominid walking along the savanna of an African valley three million years ago. You hear a rustle in the grass. Is it just the wind or is it a dangerous predator? Your answer could mean life or death."

If we fail to make the connection to a potential predator, we become the beast's dinner and are naturally selected out of the gene pool. But if we make a connection and it just turns out to be the wind, no problem—just a quick rush of adrenalin and we hurry on our way, only more alert. What is important, however, is that we quickly made a linkage.

True pattern recognition can save our life, but overly active pattern finding tends to have little impact. Thus, our ability to make quick associations survived the process of natural selection.

That's why, Shermer writes, "Our brains are belief engines: evolved pattern-recognition machines that connect the dots and create meaning out of the patterns that we think we see." "We are," he continues, "the descendants of those who were most successful at finding patterns. This process is called association learning and is fundamental to all animal behavior, from *C. elegans* to *H. sapiens.* I call this process patternicity, or the tendency to find meaningful patterns in both meaningful and meaningless noise."

Quick, illusory connections

We are oblivious to how we make quick connections from sparse information, because it is hardwired into our perception of the world. Eye physiology tells us we can only see what is right in front of us, and only see one color at a time. The rest is a colorless blur. But that's not how we perceive the world we live in.

We also have a literal blind spot where our retina is. But we don't notice it, because our brain fills in the blind spot based on detail from the surrounding area. What we think we are seeing is not literally what we are seeing. Our mind makes up for the sparse data by filling in the blanks with memories and assumptions.

Nick Chater, in his excellent book *The Mind is Flat*, writes, "our beliefs about what we see, whether we are looking at text, objects, faces or colors, are systematically misleading: we see far, far less than we think we do. Indeed, we see the world one snippet at a time; and we can tie snippets together, just as we can link together successive sentences in a story. So the 'inner world' of your current sensory experience is also, it turns out, entirely fake." This fakeness, he suggests, extends to how we think and reason.

Using patterns as shorthand

We use patterns, and expectations of patterns, as a shortcut that enables us to work effectively with the thin information we perceive. Read the phrases in this diagram.

Adapted from *Psychology of Intelligence Analysis*, Richards J. Heuer.

Simple, right? Paris in the Spring, Once in a lifetime, Bird in the hand.

But look again: the articles "the" and "a" appear twice in each phrase. Our brains focus on the expected sequence and ignore the extra information—the evidence that is extraneous to the pattern.

There is a classic study which underscores how we default to patterns, and struggle to escape them. In this research by Jerome Bruner and Leo Postman, people were exposed to cards. Some of them were the usual cards: black spades, red hearts, black clubs and red diamonds. But some of the cards messed with the pattern. There were also black hearts, red clubs and black diamonds.

Pictures of these cards were briefly flashed on the screen and people were asked to identify them. People were good with the ones that fit the pattern. But they struggled with ones that defied expectations. Black hearts and red spades were very difficult to identify—even the second time around. It took extra effort, and even then, people found it frustrating, even confounding. "I don't know what the hell it is now, not even for sure whether it's a playing card," one bewildered respondent exclaimed.

We use patterns to process information quickly and efficiently. When the expected patterns are not confirmed, we struggle. Information that runs contrary to the anticipated patterns confuses us.

Yearning for patterns

Gambling is an industry that generates around $500 billion dollars a year—and that's just the legal side of it. The amount of money spent on gambling is a powerful reminder of how compelling our tendency to see non-existent patterns is. And there is evidence that habitual gamblers have greater susceptibility to see patterns in randomness.

Wolfgang Gaissmaier and others conducted a study which asked, "Why do people gamble? A large body of research suggests that cognitive distortions play an important role in pathological gambling. Many of these distortions are specific cases of a more general misperception of randomness, specifically of an illusory perception of patterns in random sequences…. Gamblers are particularly prone to perceiving illusory patterns."

The authors "compared habitual gamblers to a matched sample of community members." They found that habitual gamblers were more susceptible to seeing patterns that did not exist, and that "gamblers are more willing to bet impulsively on perceived illusory patterns." The exploitation of the tendency to see patterns where none exist is reinforced by occasional dopamine rushes when players randomly win. It is sobering to think how much money has been squandered on illusory patterns. But it is even more sobering when we see how this pattern-seeking tendency can go even further awry.

Pattern-seeking out of control

John Nash won a Nobel Prize for his work on game theory. He also made important contributions to differential geometry and the study of partial differential equations. He was a genius who could see patterns in mathematics that others could not. Unfortunately, he also saw all sorts of other patterns. A schizophrenic, he believed, among other things, that all men with red ties were part of a communist conspiracy. He is best known as the subject of the book and movie *A Beautiful Mind*. Pattern-seeking gone amiss made his life a difficult one.

Psychologist Andrea Marie Kuszewski, interviewed in Michael Shermer's *Believing Brain*, said, "Schizophrenics who are delusional see patterns…all the time and think that they are relevant. Their PFC [prefrontal cortex] and ACC [anterior cingulate cortex] are not functioning to weed out the unlikely patterns, but instead see all patterns and give them equal weight for relevance."

Seeing patterns is a part of the way we are wired, but that tendency can go askew; it can cause people to throw away their savings, and can even ruin a beautiful mind. What effect can it have on our research?

Making linkages and generating answers

Years of studies in behavioral economics and psychology have demonstrated that most of the decisions we make are emotional and non-conscious. They are decisions made by what Nobel Laureate Daniel Kahneman calls System 1 thinking—fast, intuitive and emotional. Yet when we are asked to explain our decisions, we immediately and effortlessly produce an answer—even though the decisions were not conscious ones. We search through our store of socially acceptable explanations to concoct an answer that will satisfy the questioner, and we're not even aware of it.

"The parallel with perception is striking:" Chater writes, "we glimpse the external world through an astonishingly narrow window, and…the illusion of sensory richness is sustained by our ability to conjure up an answer, almost instantly, to almost any question that occurs to us. Now we should suspect that the apparent richness of our inner world has the same origin: as we ask questions of ourselves, answers naturally and fluently appear. Our beliefs, desires, hopes and fears do not wait pre-formed in a vast mental ante-chamber, until they are ushered one by one into the bright light of verbal expression. The left-brain interpreter constructs our thoughts and feelings at the very moment that we think and feel them."

Bad connections and not noticing

Our ability to effortlessly (and incorrectly) explain our beliefs is wonderfully illustrated by a classic study by psychologists Richard Nisbett and Timothy Wilson. They set up in a department store and invited consumers to tell them which of four pairs of pantyhose they preferred and why. People picked their favorites and explained why they liked the color or texture or whatever it was they said drove their preference. The only thing was, the stockings were identical. There were no differences. There was no rationale for picking one over another. Yet people were happy to articulate a rationale.

These findings on how quick we are to unknowingly give illusory reasons have been elaborated on in a series of elegant experiments by Swedish psychologists Petter Johansson, Lars Hall and others at the Choice Blindness Lab at Sweden's Lund University. In one study, they showed people two pictures of people's faces and asked them to choose which of the two they found more attractive. The interviewer then, by sleight of hand, handed respondents the picture of the person they had picked as being less attractive and asked them why they had chosen this person as being more attractive.

Only a quarter of the people spotted the "mistake." The rest of them went blithely on to offer detailed explanations as to why they chose the person whose picture they were now seeing again—completely oblivious to the fact they were making up their reasoning as they went along. Johansson and Hall have seen similar results in studies of political choice, taste tests, and more. People will be unaware of the switch and easily explain "why" they made the choices they, in fact, did not make.

This has important implications for the questions we ask. We know that questions like "why" will generate misleading but socially acceptable answers. And the person giving the reasons will be completely unaware that they are making it up as they go along.

WYSIATI

WYSIATI is a word coined by Daniel Kahneman. It is an acronym for What You See Is All There Is. Kahneman uses it to describe our tendency to make snap judgements based on very little information. For example, when we first meet someone, we size them up and make a judgement about all sorts of things about them within a second. Of course, we know very little about that person, but our minds are happy to jump to a conclusion based on only the scantest of information.

Kahneman described WYSIATI this way in an interview with Inc television: "If I tell you 'here is a leader of the nation and she is intelligent and strong.' Now if I ask you at this point 'Is she a good leader?' You already have an answer." The interviewer nodded yes. Kahneman continued, "Now the third word could be corrupt. I hadn't told you anything about her character. You were not waiting. You took the information you had and made the best story possible out of it. That's the way our mind works. We construct stories out of evidence that is very slight, very partial, could be biased—but we make the best story possible out of it. That's the way System 1 is wired."

"System 1 is a storyteller," Kahneman explained in an interview for an American Psychological Association publication. "It tells the best stories that it can from the information available, even when the information is sparse or unreliable. And that makes stories that are based on very different qualities of evidence equally compelling. Our measure of how 'good' a story is—how confident we are in its accuracy—is not an evaluation of the reliability of the evidence and its quality, it's a measure of the coherence of the story."

"People are designed to tell the best story possible. So WYSIATI means that we use the information we have as if it is the only information. We don't spend much time saying, 'Well, there is much we don't know.' We make do with what we do know. And that concept is very central to the functioning of our mind."

This poses a real challenge for insights professionals because it makes it all too easy to assume we know the answer even if we don't have the full picture. It's effortlessly natural to fill in the blanks and assume the patterns we intuit are right.

Seeing spurious connections in data

Our tendency to seek and find patterns in random (and sparse) information is why we see faces in clouds and the Virgin Mary on toast. iPhone sales are almost perfectly correlated (.999) with the number of people who died from falling down the stairs, over the same time period, in the U.S. and U.K. Now, if your mind went to people falling down the stairs because they were focused on their iPhone instead of perambulating, then you just experienced this desire to find linkages even when they don't exist.

iPhone sales are also almost equally perfectly correlated with the consumption of American cheese; U.S. spending on science, space and technology; and attendance at Disney World's Animal Kingdom, according to data you can analyze at the entertaining website Spurious Correlations. And while those examples are obviously ridiculous, the same thing can happen in any analysis, especially if we focus our attention on tests of statistical significance.

En garde

We must be on guard and conscious of how our pattern-making brains complicate both survey design and our analysis. We need to be acutely conscious that we are hardwired, as both respondents and analysts, to make connections and see patterns where there are none.

Now take this pattern-seeking tendency and mix it with a good dose of misunderstanding and we get the toxic misapplication of "statistical significance"—a problem that has been bedeviling science in general, and the insights profession in particular, for many years.

Chapter 5: The danger of relying on statistical significance

"Do not put your faith in what statistics say until you have carefully considered what they do not say."
William W. Watt

"Is that statistically significant?"

This question sounds scientific and well meaning, but is too often misguided and dangerous, according to leading statisticians. The popular misconception that statistical significance is the mark of truth has many unintended consequences. The biggest problem is that often what appears to be fact is simply statistical noise, and what may well be fact is sadly ignored.

The problem is not so much with the statistical tools, but rather how they are applied. You've probably seen data tables in which every column is compared to every other column, usually at a 95% confidence interval. "Significant" differences are noted with a letter or number. Each table can have 100 or more tests. Researchers often scour the tables looking for "significant" differences and then try to explain the differences. This is where the trouble begins.

Most people are familiar with the idea that one in twenty of these tests will yield a false positive—suggesting there is a difference when none exists. But the reality is that the error rate is much higher, particularly when there are multiple comparisons involved and the tools are used in ways they were never intended to be used.

"Most scientists would look at...[a] p-value of 0.01 and say that there was just a 1% chance of this result being a false alarm. But they would be wrong," statistician Regina Nuzzo writes in *Nature*. "The p-value cannot say this: all it can do is summarize the data assuming a specific null hypothesis. It cannot work backward and make statements about the underlying reality. That requires another piece of information: the odds that a real effect was there in the first place."

She goes on to say, "According to one widely used calculation, a p-value of 0.01 corresponds to a false-alarm probability of at least 11%, depending on the underlying probability that there is a true effect; a p-value of 0.05 raises that chance to at least 29%."

Replication crisis in academia

It has been the convention to use a 95% confidence interval ($p \leq 0.05$) as a marker of truth not only in the world of market research but in the scientific community in general. Journals are generally not interested in publishing studies in which the results are not "significant." And academics need to publish to get promoted or even stay employed. The result has been a disaster for science.

There is plenty of evidence to suggest that many published papers have findings that cannot be reproduced because of a misuse of statistical testing. The journals *Nature* and *Science* are very prestigious, and academics clamor to have their papers accepted by them. But a study published in *Nature* entitled "Evaluating the replicability of social science experiments in *Nature* and *Science* between 2010 and 2015" reported the authors were able to replicate only six in 10 of them, and the effect size of the replications was "on average about 50% of the original effect size."

Similarly dismal measures of reproducibility and replicability have been reported in many other fields, including psychology, economics, and medicine. One high profile casualty of a misguided focus on "significant findings" is American researcher and professor Brian Wansink.

His research focused on how people make food choices, and he is the author of the bestselling books *Mindless Eating* and *Slim by Design*. His work popularized the ideas that plate size and color influence how much you eat and that 100 calorie packages reduce the amount overweight people eat. Many problems were later discovered with

Wansink's work, but what first got people looking into his work was his uncritical use of statistical tests, or "p-hacking." He was caught out after publicly encouraging graduate students and collaborators to troll through data sets looking for "statistically significant" findings, rather than following the scientific process of testing predetermined hypotheses.

According to Tim Vanderzee, a researcher who investigated Wansink's work, there are alleged problems with 52 of his publications, which have been cited over 4,000 times in 25 different journals and in eight books. When evidence of his unscientific approach surfaced, his university suspended him from teaching and ultimately released him. Misuse of statistical testing can have dire effects.

As researchers, we seek to inform and guide decision making. Uncritical use of stats testing can result in us misleading and misinforming instead. That's a situation no one wants. So, what's a researcher to do?

Fortunately, the American Statistical Association (ASA) has some advice.

Use and abuse of significance testing

The ASA put out a formal statement on the use and misuse of p-values. They set forth "principles underlying the proper use and interpretation of the p-value." They state, "The widespread use of 'statistical significance' (generally interpreted as 'p ≤ 0.05') as a license for making a claim of a scientific finding (or implied truth) leads to considerable distortion of the scientific process. A conclusion does not immediately become 'true' on one side of the divide and 'false' on the other."

They suggest, "Researchers should recognize that a p-value without context or other evidence provides limited information." They counsel that researchers "should bring many contextual factors into play to derive scientific inferences, including the design of a study, the quality of the measurements, the external evidence for the phenomenon under study, and the validity of assumptions that underlie the data analysis." They conclude that good statistical practice emphasizes "understanding of the phenomenon under study, interpretation of results in context, complete reporting and proper logical and quantitative understanding of what data summaries mean. No single index should substitute for scientific reasoning." Context is truly the antidote.

Statisticians are also warning against thinking too narrowly about what a p-value can reveal. A comment in *Nature* by Valentin Amrhein, Sander Greenland, Blake McShane, and more than 800 other signatories points to the reduction of a p-value to a significant/not significant dichotomy as a big part of the problem. They write, "we are not advocating a ban on p values, confidence intervals or other statistical measures — only that we should not treat them categorically. This includes dichotomization as statistically significant or not, as well as categorization based on other statistical measures such as Bayes factors.

"One reason to avoid such 'dichotomania' is that all statistics, including p-values and confidence intervals, naturally vary from study to study, and often do so to a surprising degree. In fact, random variation alone can easily lead to large disparities in p values, far beyond falling just to either side of the 0.05 threshold. For example, even if researchers could conduct two perfect replication studies of some genuine effect, each with 80% power (chance) of achieving $p < 0.05$, it would not be very surprising for one to obtain $p < 0.01$ and the other $p > 0.30$."

They suggest that "The trouble is human and cognitive more than it is statistical: bucketing results into 'statistically significant' and 'statistically non-significant' makes people think that the items assigned in that way are categorically different."

That kind of categorical thinking makes it easy to miss real differences and focus on false ones. A more nuanced approach to judging what is "significant" is clearly needed.

How did we get into this mess?

If our reliance on over-simplified "significance" testing is a problem, how the heck did we end up here? Incredibly, the story involves two statisticians who despised each other and ended up with their ideas mashed together in an unholy alliance that neither approved of. And it all started with a cup of tea in 1920's England.

A group of academics had gathered for tea. One was Dr. Blanche Bristol who, when offered a cup of tea by a colleague, turned it down. The trouble was the man poured the tea into the cup first, then added the milk. Dr. Bristol rejected it because she preferred the milk to be poured into the cup first, and the tea afterward. The man who had poured the tea suggested she surely could not tell the difference. She insisted she could. The man, Dr. Ronald Aylmer Fisher, went on to become a seminal statistician. He proposed a test, which he famously described in his book *The Design of Experiments*. He would prepare eight cups of tea: four with the tea poured first and four with the milk poured first. She had to guess which was which.

His innovation in designing this experiment was to propose the null hypothesis—that she would be unable to guess them all correctly. Fisher calculated that her chance of guessing all cups correctly was 1/70. He was provisionally willing to concede her ability (rejecting the null hypothesis) in this case only. She, reportedly, got them all correct. The null hypothesis was rejected. Thus began significance testing.

Meanwhile, two competing statisticians, Jerzy Neyman and Ergon Pearson, were working on hypothesis testing—selecting among competing hypotheses based on the experimental evidence alone. Neyman suggested that hypothesis testing was an improvement on significance testing. That did not sit well with Fisher. He disliked Neyman because he had worked with Pearson's father, with whom Fisher had a long-running disagreement. Fisher and Neyman battled over which method was better until Fisher's death.

The null ritual

In the meantime, something odd happened. Gerd Gigerenzer sums it up rather nicely in his (wryly caustic) paper "Statistical Rituals: The Replication Delusion and How We Got There": "Early textbook writers struggled to create a supposedly objective method of statistical inference that would distinguish a cause from a chance in a mechanical way, eliminating judgment. The result was a shotgun wedding between some of Fisher's ideas and those of his intellectual opponents, the Polish statistician Jerzy Neyman (1894–1981) and the British statistician Egon

S. Pearson (1895–1980). The essence of this hybrid theory is the null ritual."

He describes what he calls the "null ritual" this way:

"1. Set up a null hypothesis of 'no mean difference' or 'zero correlation.' Do not specify the predictions of your own research hypothesis.

2. Use 5% as a convention for rejecting the null hypothesis. If the test is significant, accept your research hypothesis. Report the test result as p < .05, p < .01, or p < .001, whichever level is met by the obtained p-value.

3. Always perform this procedure."

"The null ritual does not exist in statistics proper," Gigerenzer continues. "This point is not always understood; even its critics sometimes confuse it with Fisher's theory of null-hypothesis testing and call it 'null-hypothesis significance testing.' In fact, the ritual is an incoherent mishmash of ideas from Fisher on the one hand and Neyman and Pearson on the other, spiked with a characteristically novel contribution: the elimination of researchers' judgment."

The way forward

We find ourselves in a situation where uncritical use of a bastardized test has led to a "replication crisis" in science and the misuse and abuse of the notion of significance. We need to rethink how we use significance testing.

Firstly, we need to take a finding of "significance" with a grain of salt. The error rate is larger than is commonly assumed. Secondly, we need to stay away from data fishing: trolling for "significant" differences. Thirdly, we need to understand that something which might not pass the significance test might be meaningful. Fourthly, we need to consider context. As the ASA recommends, "no single index should substitute for scientific reasoning."

So next time someone asks, "Is that statistically significant?" we should consider whether that is the right question. A better question would be "are the differences meaningful?"

Asking this would steer us away from the trap of binary thinking and guide us toward contextualizing a finding in a world rich with information.

Chapter 6: Who, me biased?

"The mind of man is far from the nature of a clear and equal glass, wherein the beams of things should reflect according to their true incidence; nay, it is rather like an enchanted glass, full of superstition and imposture...."
Francis Bacon

A whiff of history

My dog can smell time. Her understanding of scents is so fine-tuned that she can determine how long it has been since a smell was laid down. Every scent tells her something about what happened earlier. Imagine walking out of your home and being able to see who had been by, and how long ago. An equivalent for us would be if we could see gradually fading traces of people and strollers and cars and bikes and where they had been and gone.

The ability to smell recent history is something we don't have. We're oblivious to it. And dogs can hear sounds that we have no idea are even being generated. We are deaf to them. And while my dog is pretty amazing, she can also be blinded by her own biases and assumptions.

There is a grey cat on our street that bullies all the other cats, and she torments all the dogs. She even bothers the elderly lady who lives in the house next to her. This cat is a piece of work.

The cat sometimes sits under a car in the driveway next door to our house. And, once in a blue moon, when I take my dog out for a walk, the cat will be there sitting under the car glowering at everything that passes. That's when my dog tries to rip my arm out of its socket while she lunges for the cat, who simply yawns and looks bored because she knows my dog is far too big to get under the car.

After the dog saw the cat under the car a few times, she took to coming out of the house and wanting to look underneath the car before proceeding down the street. Ninety-nine percent of the time the cat is not there. But my dog looks anyways.

Occasionally I'll spot the cat across the street. But my dog, so intent on checking under the car, will be oblivious to the cat. And I, of course, will be blissfully unaware of the history of who has just walked past, and I'll miss everything happening in the frequencies I can't hear. We all have our blind spots.

Cognitive biases

When we think of cognitive biases, we typically focus on what they mean for respondents. Can people really tell us about a choice they made when using fast, intuitive System 1 thinking, when they are unaware of it? Will anchoring effects from a prior question influence how they answer our next question? Will recent events warp how people answer questions about what they usually do?

These are all important considerations when designing studies. But equally vital is reflection on how cognitive biases affect our analysis and insight generation.

Cognitive biases are brain processes that can lead us to make mistakes in how we think. These biases are mainly the result of shortcuts our brains take to react quickly and limitations in our processing power. We like to think we can comprehend all, make unbiased judgements, and analyze information in ways that are impartial and completely accurate. But science tells us otherwise. We're human. And being human means being subject to limitations and biases.

Sam Reimer is a professor of sociology at Crandall University. In his upper level methods course he likes to point out the limits of our cognitive abilities. "I talk about how we think about knowledge in general. I talk about critical realism, and what can we really know? Can our senses really tell us everything? How fallible is our knowledge?" He says, "Part of my larger task is to encourage them to think carefully about the world around them." He wants to ensure his students go forth aware of their limitations and biases.

In the worlds of intelligence analysis, medicine, and law there are many examples which poignantly reveal how unchecked biases in analysis and data collection can lead to wars, fatal medical errors, and wrongful convictions. In the realm of insights, the implications are not so dire, but they are no less common and no less malignant.

Just can't help myself

The thing about cognitive bias is that you can't avoid it. You can be aware of it. You can try to mitigate it. But you can't stop it from happening.

Perceptual illusions are the visual cousins of cognitive biases. We experience them, but we can't get past them—even when we are conscious of them. Consider the arrows below. The lines are identical in length. The only difference is the direction of the arrows on the ends.

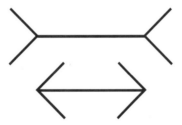

Do they look the same? I know they are the same, because measuring them confirms that they are the same length. But do they look the same? Not to me, no matter how hard I look. Or how much I am acutely aware they are the same. This illusion has been fooling people ever since German sociologist Franz Carl Müller-Lyer first devised it in 1889.

"We're a bit freaked out by really good optical illusions because they force us to directly confront a reality we tend to ignore as we go through our daily lives," writes Steven Novella in *The Skeptics' Guide to the Universe*. "What we think we see is not objective; it is a process of our brains, and that process can be fooled."

Hence the Dutch artist M.C. Escher played with worlds in which everything appeared logical and connected, and yet simultaneously defied logic. In his famous print *Ascending and Descending*, two sets of people are trudging forever upwards and eternally downwards on an impossible four-sided eternal staircase. It was produced in 1960, but its enduring power to confound is such that posters of it still adorn dorm rooms today. We know it doesn't make sense, and yet it does. Such is the nature of our perceptions.

I knew it was confirmation bias

We are hard-wired to have cognitive biases. It's the way our brains function. Cognitive biases help us make quick decisions about almost everything we do, including which way to turn when we get out of the elevator. But sometimes they lead us the wrong way.

There are at least 288 known cognitive biases—covering everything from anchoring to the Zeigarnik effect. But a European Union project undertaken by a consortium of intelligence agencies singled out 29 that influenced intelligence analysis in everything from research design to analysis and reporting. Chief among them is confirmation bias: "the tendency to search for, interpret, favor, and recall information in a way that affirms one's prior beliefs or hypotheses."

Confirmation bias is not newly discovered. It was what Julius Caesar was talking about when he said, "Men in general are quick to believe that which they wish to be true," and what Voltaire was speaking about when he quipped that "The human brain is a complex organ with the wonderful power of enabling man to find reasons for continuing to believe whatever it is that he wants to believe."

It's a bias that can have deadly effects.

Stalin's confirmation bias makes Germany's attack a crippling "surprise"

Joseph Stalin, who ruled the Soviet Union from the mid–1920s until 1953, allowed confirmation bias to blind himself—and the Soviet military—to the fact that, in 1941, Hitler would violate a non-aggression pact and invade the Soviet Union.

Stalin assumed Germany would avoid a war on two fronts at the same time: the U.K. and the Soviet Union. Stalin knew Hitler had his hands full trying to bomb Great Britain into submission. He could not imagine that Hitler would quickly attack the Soviet Union too—especially when they had an agreement.

When clear evidence suggested otherwise, he interpreted it in a way that affirmed his prior assumptions. We do that too, only millions of people don't die. We, as insights professionals, can just end up giving advice that will misguide our stakeholders.

In his book *Challenges in Intelligence Analysis: Lessons from 1300 BCE to the Present*, ex-CIA analyst and professor of intelligence analysis Timothy Walton eloquently describes this cautionary tale. Stalin, he writes, "assumed that any German attack would be preceded by an ultimatum. To support his assessment, Stalin could draw on the reassuring tone of the remarks that were being made by the German ambassador to Moscow. Stalin did not realize, however, that the ambassador was not part of Hitler's inner circle, and thus was not a reliable source regarding the German leader's intentions."

When the U.S. warned Stalin that they had intercepted communications that revealed Germany was preparing to invade the Soviet Union, Stalin wrote it off as "provocation" on the part of the Americans. When the U.K. offered similar warnings, he assumed they were just trying to goad Russia into war with Germany so that the U.K. would find some relief from Germany's relentless attacks. Stalin was also getting mixed reports from Soviet Intelligence. So, he favored the data that supported his prior assumptions.

"There were also indications that Hitler wanted to forge a great continental diplomatic bloc, including the USSR, that would convince the British that is was impossible for them to find allies; and therefore they could come with an agreement with Germany to end the war," Walton writes. "Naturally, Stalin gave great credence to reports, like these, that confirmed his preconceptions."

When a prized Soviet intelligence source—a spy who worked for the German Ministry of Aviation—reported that the Air Force was "convinced that the issue of the attack by Germany on the Soviet Union is definitely decided," Stalin wrote it off as "disinformation."

Early in the morning of June 22, 1941, Soviet trains continued to cross the border delivering supplies to the German Army. Meanwhile, German commanders ready to give the order to attack witnessed the Soviets' obliviousness with stunned disbelief. Minutes later, the Germans opened fire.

"Even as the first reports came in of guns firing, instructions from the Soviet military command, still operating in Stalin's framework, saw the German actions as unprovoked and minor, rather than as indicators of war....In the months that followed, massive losses of Soviet men and equipment would be one of the greatest defeats in history," Walton explains.

"Stalin's role as dictator required him to appear all-knowing and infallible, but his shortcomings as an analyst demonstrate many of the cognitive pitfalls that analysts face. These included...giving more credence to reports that confirm one's point of view while undervaluing contradictory information," according to Professor Walton.

In the insights industry, our cognitive biases can also cause us to misinterpret the information we have. It won't lead to war, but it will have very real commercial repercussions for the organizations we serve.

Heal me, please

We count on physicians to save lives. But when cognitive biases get in the way, people can die. Consider a case recounted in "From

Mindlessness to Mindful Practice—Cognitive Bias and Clinical Decision Making," by Dr. Pat Croskerry.

An 18-year-old woman is referred by her family doctor to psychiatry for symptoms of severe anxiety and depression. She has been experiencing frequent episodes of shortness of breath, cramps in her hands and feet, and loss of consciousness. The admitting psychiatrist wants to rule out a respiratory problem, so he sends her to the emergency department for an X-ray to check for pneumonia.

The patient is obese, has asthma, and smokes. Her complaint is that she is breathless; otherwise, she is not in distress. Her chest exam is normal. So is the blood work and chest X-ray. The doctor "believes the patient can be safely returned to the psychiatric facility. He attributes her respiratory problems to anxiety."

"While she awaits transfer, she becomes very agitated and short of breath. Several nurses attempt to settle her, encouraging her to breathe into a paper bag" (which is standard treatment for people hyperventilating due to panic or anxiety). Shortly afterward she loses consciousness and, despite heroic efforts, dies.

"The autopsy shows she had an infected blood clot in her pelvis that cut off her blood flow and therefore her ability to breathe normally. She had multiple older clots, indicating this was not the first time she had suffered such a blockage.

"Several cognitive failures probably influence the outcome in this case," Dr. Croskerry writes. "The patient's diagnosis of anxiety established 'momentum'...and although she may have had hyperventilation due to anxiety, other possibilities were not ruled out earlier on in her care." The focus on her anxiety led physicians to ignore other possible causes for her breathing problems.

Confirmation bias can kill. But it can also leave you rotting in jail.

You got the wrong guy

Criminal justice is another area where cognitive biases can have profoundly negative effects. In the paper "Confirmation Bias and Other Systemic Causes of Wrongful Convictions: A Sentinel Events Perspective," a study of 50 cases of wrongful convictions, criminology professors Kim Rossmo and Joycelyn Pollock report that confirmation bias was a driving factor in three quarters of the cases, while "tunnel vision" was implicated in half. These cognitive failures were also linked to other problems, like "a rush to judgement" and "improper interrogations."

The results can be tragic.

One of the cases analyzed by Rossmo and Pollock is that of Bruce Lisker. Lisker was just 17 and high on methamphetamines when he came home and discovered his mother stabbed to death. He immediately called 911. When medics arrived, his hands were covered with blood.

"The first detective on the scene knew Bruce from prior interactions and considered him a 'punk.' Investigators coerced a confession (quickly recanted) from the 17-year-old teenager through the offer of a plea bargain," Rossmo and Pollock reported. "A rush to judgment followed by tunnel vision led to confirmation bias. Exculpatory evidence was ignored, while the alibi of an alternative and viable suspect was never checked despite inconsistencies in his story."

Bruce rotted in jail for 26 years before it was determined that he was innocent and that someone else had killed his mother. At age 43, he emerged from prison all too aware of the impact cognitive biases can have on how we view information and make judgements.

Confirmation bias and insights

It is relatively easy to spot confirmation bias in others. Ever been to a focus group where the product manager spends most of the session complaining that these respondents "are not the right people" when they say things that run contrary to her expectations? Or seizes on the one thing that confirms her assumptions while ignoring the rest of what was said? It happens all the time.

The same thing happens with insights professionals. It's just harder to detect in ourselves. It's very easy to gravitate toward information that "makes sense" and gloss over or outright ignore data that doesn't fit with our current view of the market.

We'll leave the last word on confirmation bias to comedian Jon Ronson: "Ever since I first learned about confirmation bias, I've been seeing it everywhere."

Chapter 7: Light at the end of the tunnel

"It is that which we do know which is the great hindrance to our learning, not that which we do not know."
Claude Bernard

Tunnel vision is a pernicious bias. It leads us to conclusions that feel right but are wrong. Tunnel vision gives us answers we expect, while obscuring the truth.

Tunnel vision is linked to confirmation bias, hindsight bias and outcome bias. WYSIATI can also be involved, as people grapple with scant data. And belief persistence bias—where people cling to their original conclusions despite contradictory evidence—is also a factor.

Hindsight bias is the tendency to see events that have already occurred as being more predictable than they were before they happened. It's the "knew-it-all-along" effect. Hindsight bias results in an oversimplification of the past and the ignoring of the reality of uncertainty, doubt, and complication. But you already knew that, right?

Outcome bias comes in when we judge a result by what happened rather than how we got there. It leads people to ignore randomness and other factors and results in an over-simplification. Let's say your friend does well in real estate, so you decide to invest in it too. It just seems like an obviously good idea. But have you thought about how the economy is doing, how much housing stock is being built, and what the demographic trends are? Are they the same as when your friend made her money? Outcome bias leads us to oversimplify problems and make poor choices as a result.

Beware the tunnel

Tunnel vision is dangerous because it can direct us to find what we expect, rather than what is real. And it can cause us to oversimply and be certain of our incorrect conclusions. When, after the presentation of research results, the product manager says, "that's what I expected," you must wonder if you or they—or indeed both of you—were the victims of tunnel vision. It is an important question to ask, because tunnel vision can have powerfully misleading effects. It shows up very tragically in the world of policing and justice.

Many wrongful convictions can be traced to tunnel vision—with police and prosecutors assuming they have identified the perpetrator. They then end up focusing on evidence that supports that conviction, at the expense of ignoring other findings that would reveal that they had come to the wrong conclusion.

Law professors Keith Findlay and Michael Scott wrote a classic paper entitled "The Multiple Dimensions of Tunnel Vision in Criminal Cases." Keith Findlay is a former public defender who teaches at the University of Wisconsin Law School. He was co-founder of the Wisconsin Innocence Project. Michael Scott is a former police chief with a law degree from Harvard who teaches at Arizona State University. He is the director of Center for Problem-Oriented Policing.

They define tunnel vision as a "'compendium of common heuristics and logical fallacies,' to which we are all susceptible, that lead actors in the criminal justice system to 'focus on a suspect, select and filter the evidence that will "build a case" for conviction, while ignoring or suppressing evidence that points away from guilt.' This process leads investigators, prosecutors, judges, and defense lawyers alike to focus on a particular conclusion and then filter all evidence in a case through the lens provided by that conclusion. Through that filter, all information supporting the adopted conclusion is elevated in significance, viewed as consistent with the other evidence, and deemed relevant and probative. Evidence inconsistent with the chosen theory is easily overlooked or dismissed as irrelevant, incredible, or unreliable."

Making a murderer

One high-profile wrongful conviction is the case of Steven Avery, popularized in the Netflix series Making a Murderer. Findlay and Scott address this case and write, "Avery was wrongly convicted because tunnel vision prevented system actors from considering alternative theories about the crime until DNA evidence finally proved in 2003 that Avery was innocent, and that another man, Gregory Allen, was guilty. By then Avery had served more than eighteen years in prison."

Steven Avery, said to have an IQ of seventy, struggled in school and fell in with the wrong crowd. At 18 he was convicted of burgling a bar. A year later he was arrested for animal cruelty after dousing his cat in gasoline and directing a friend to set it on fire. Three years after that, he ran his cousin's car off the side of the road and pointed a gun at her. In addition to being his cousin, she was the wife of a county deputy. Mr. Avery did not have a good reputation where he lived in Manitowoc County, Wisconsin.

Not long after the incident with Avery's cousin, a young woman was brutally sexually assaulted while jogging on a Manitowoc County beach. Avery was arrested after the victim picked him from an array of photos, and later from a live lineup. This was despite the fact that Avery was 40 miles away in Green Bay shortly after the attack with his family of five, including 6-day old twins. He had 16 witnesses and an alibi supported by a time-stamped store receipt. But he was charged and convicted of rape and attempted murder and sentenced to 32 years.

"While being treated in the hospital after the attack," write Findlay and Scott, "the victim gave police a description of her attacker and helped create a composite sketch. Based on that description and sketch, local sheriff's deputies thought the attacker might be Avery."

"The sheriff presented Avery's photo to the victim as part of a nine-photo simultaneous array, telling her that 'the suspect might be in there,'" Findlay and Scott report. "The victim later said the sheriff's statement led her to 'believe that the suspect's photograph was included in the group of nine photos.' However, a photograph of Allen, the true perpetrator, was not included in the array and the victim instead selected Avery's photo."

A few days later, the victim identified Avery out of a lineup in which he was the only one whose picture had also been in the photo array. He was also the shortest, youngest, and fairest person in the line-up, which included people wearing glasses and people dressed in professional attire and wearing ties.

Round up the usual suspects

I spoke with a New York City detective, who has been granted anonymity because he was not authorized to speak publicly for this book. He is all too aware of the limitations of identification and just how easy it is for confirmation bias to creep in. He said, "Say you got robbed on the corner of 58th Street and Lexington Avenue. I know a guy who does robberies over there all the time. I'm going to have the victim look at a lineup that's got Mickey in it, because Mickey did a robbery over there three weeks ago, and I bet he did this one, too.

"So, I put Mickey in there. Mickey looks kind of like it. And the victim says, 'Well, yeah. Number four looks kind of good'. Then it's like, all right. Number four it is. It's Mickey. So, that was the standard, and obviously it's a terrible standard. That's why you get a lot of these bad ID's. You show people mugshots. I've had people pick out people from mugshots who were in jail at the time of the incident. They're positive that's the guy, and you'll go 'this guy was on Rikers Island when this happened.' I've just seen so many people picking people who were in jail, out of the country, in a different state. It's just such an unreliable metric." What he prefers and is finding increasingly accessible is video footage, which is an important new data source for detectives.

It sounds a bit ridiculous to be using unreliable techniques which are vulnerable to confirmation bias. You might think it's something we'd never do in the world of insights. But consider this example.

Compute this

A computer manufacturer has a new laptop feature that their R&D department has invested heavily in. The product manager wants to get feedback on how important this new feature is, and she approaches the insights team to conduct some focus groups with tech enthusiasts. At the groups, people enthuse about the new feature, and the product manager and R&D team sit happily in the backroom, sipping lite beer and red wine and contentedly popping M&Ms.

The insights team know that a focus group is not reliable all on its own, so they do a quick concept test on the new feature with a similar cohort of people interested in technology. The results are pretty good, with very high likeability scores. Compared to concepts they have tested before, this new feature does slightly better than average. The product manager uses the results of the focus group and concept test as a rationale for heavily promoting the new feature. Sound familiar?

Because of the amount of money and time invested in the new feature, the investigation is practically dripping in confirmation bias right from the start, not to mention sunk cost bias. Focus groups are well understood to suffer from groupthink and social desirability bias, not to mention providing very small and generally unrepresentative samples of people willing to give up their evening to talk about your product.

Stock the groups with tech enthusiasts and ask how important the feature is and, guess what, tech enthusiasts are enthusiastic. By focusing on how important the feature is, the team has asked a System 2 logical question about a System 1 emotional reaction, thereby preordaining the answer.

People don't really know what is important, because that reaction is unconscious and emotional. But when we ask them if the feature is important, they say 'of course' because when you ask people what is important, they say everything is important.

When we ask "why" they feel it is important, their minds instantly generate a socially acceptable and logical rationale for their answers— even though we know people can't give us accurate information on why, because they are not conscious of their thought processes.

The concept test has people rate the new feature in isolation and then compares the reaction to the new feature to a database consisting mostly of concepts that were weeded out. The fact that it rates slightly above average does not mean much, but the product manager happily latches on to it because it confirms what she knew all along: this new feature is going to be great!

The product is launched with tremendous fanfare about the new feature. The market yawns, and telemetry data shows the feature isn't used very much. The feature gets quietly dropped when the next model is rolled out.

This scenario and ones like it are not unfamiliar. But they are great examples of tunnel vision in action. The tunnel vision is identifiable to an outsider, even though the product manager and R&D would probably not be conscious of it. And techniques that are known to be problematic get used. But that's okay because we're really used to doing focus groups and asking what's important—just like police are really used to using mugshots.

It gets worse

Knowing that tunnel vision is easy to find, but important to avoid, let's turn back to the case of Steven Avery. We know that, because of his recent arrest and conviction for driving a deputy's wife off the road and pulling a gun, there was availability bias happening within the sheriff's department. Avery was top of mind, and top of mind solutions are easy ones. System 1 loves easy solutions.

The police and prosecutor were so convinced by the victim identification that they had the right man that they looked for pieces of evidence to support their case, and disconfirmed information that contradicted their assumption.

"The State bolstered its eyewitness evidence with circumstantial evidence," Findlay and Scott recount. "Deputies swore that the night of the arrest they told Avery only that he was being arrested for attempted murder, yet they claimed Avery told his wife he was being accused of attempting to murder a 'girl.' Despite the ambiguous nature of that evidence, the deputies, the prosecutor, and, ultimately, the courts thought it was highly incriminating that Avery seemed to know the gender of the victim. In addition, to rebut Avery's alibi—his claim that he had spent the day pouring concrete with his extended family and friends—the State offered evidence that the State Crime Laboratory could find no concrete dust on his clothes."

Avery's defense team presented evidence that he had purchased paint in Green Bay, over an hour's drive away, at 5:13 pm—a little more than an hour after the victim said the attack had begun. The manager had the time-stamped receipt and remembered the man and his five young children, including the newborn twins.

"Sheriff's deputies countered that they had done a timed drive from the location of the assault to the Green Bay Shopko and had been able to make it to the checkout line in fifty-seven minutes," Findlay and Scott write. "But, as the Attorney General concluded after investigating Avery's wrongful conviction in 2003: '[T]he officers admitted that they went ten miles per hour over the speed limit to reach those numbers and that the officers did not account for potential delays resulting from the presence of the five children including six-day old twins, all of whom were seen with Avery and his wife at the Shopko. Moreover, the re-enactment did not allow any time for picking up Avery's family and would therefore assume that Avery's wife and five children were at the beach somewhere or in the car while he committed the assault.'

Avery always maintained his innocence. After he had languished in prison for 18 years, the Wisconsin State Crime Laboratory was able to use newly developed technology to extract DNA from the victim's pubic hair combings. That DNA profile conclusively excluded Avery, and he was released.

Findlay and Scott conclude, "simply put, tunnel vision prevented the deputies, the prosecutor, the judge and the jury from appreciating the implausibility of the scenario."

It's important to note that analyses of wrongful conviction cases very rarely turn up a cop or prosecutor out to get someone. What is almost always concluded is that confirmation bias and tunnel vision, combined with organizational pressures to get a conviction, are to blame.

"We have to remember that wrongful convictions do not happen out of malice. I have never met a policeman who has deliberately tried to frame an innocent man—this is not how wrongful convictions occur," writes P.J. Wilson in *Wrongful Convictions: Lessons Learned from the Sophonow Public*

Inquiry. "Instead, investigators become convinced of the guilt of the people…because the evidence itself appears to be so convincing. It is crucial to remember that the case against an accused, on the evidence, can be extremely compelling and yet the accused may be innocent."

Insights industry professionals can also very innocently and unwittingly be affected by tunnel vision and yet be completely convinced we have the right story.

Seeing the light

When we get affected by tunnel vision, the impact is not so visible or dramatic. It might lead to a failed product or a missed opportunity. But it's hard to quantify the economic impact of tunnel vision—mainly because it is opportunity lost. And nobody is fighting to expose the error of our ways, so it goes undetected. But that's not really an acceptable situation. We need to grapple with our biases. We need to fight back. The question is how?

The good news is we are not the first group to realize that biases—cognitive and otherwise—are preventing us from coming to full and factual insights. Other sense-makers have led the way.

Chapter 8: Navigating the way forward

"The history of science, like the history of all human ideas, is a history of irresponsible dreams, of obstinacy and of error. But science is one of the very few human activities—perhaps the only one—in which errors are systematically criticized and fairly often, in time, corrected."
Karl Popper

The journey to an insight is not straightforward. We must dodge avalanches of information, clamor over mounds of cognitive biases, and try to avoid tumbling down the chute of tunnel vision.

The promised land of insights stands in the distance, hazy but alluring. Will we fly there via art—an expression of our imagination that seeks to engage? Or do we trundle down the road of craft, using a personalized process but with a generally consistent output? Or do we ride the rails of science, where our results are reproducible and validated in terms of return on investment (ROI)?

We, like many sense-makers, aspire to science. But we are not quite there. Yes, we use elements of science, sometimes well and sometimes poorly, but to say that the insights industry today is scientific would be to stretch the term to the point of tearing. We rarely bother to test for reproducibility. And validation through ROI is our unacknowledged Achille's heel.

The world of insights uses elements of art—a phrase that speaks volumes, a metaphor that drives the point home, or a visualization that makes connections clear—but insights professionals do not just offer up individualistic remixes of information. We're too nerdy for that.

We certainly do approach research as a craft. We do studies, very similar to each other, but slightly different every time. Each person puts a different spin on their approach, often influenced by whom they first worked with, or whom they share tips and tricks with. There is great pride in being a fine craftsperson, but there is also great risk. Sources of information that provide greater efficiency, reliability, and proven return on investment will win the day. Just ask a cordwainer, if you can find one.

Cordwainers craft handmade shoes, as opposed to cobblers, who repair them. Once all shoes were individually crafted, but the efficiency of industrial production—with all its limitations—has won the day. Shoes are mass produced, but in seemingly infinite variety. Occasionally we need a cobbler to repair one. But the days of master cordwainers are done.

Arts and crafts and science

What we do in the world of insights involves elements of art, craft and science. But we can't keep doing it the way we have always done it. There are so many sources of information that can guide decision making that if we don't continue to evolve with the times, some other groups will take our place as the source of insights. Cordwainers were replaced by designers, engineers, marketers and logistics experts. But we are uniquely positioned to own the insights domain, provided we think beyond the survey and embrace all streams of information, and can turn the generation of insights into an efficient, reliable, and profit-producing process. We are, of course, not alone in this type of journey.

Rob Johnston is an ethnographer with a focus on the anthropology of work. He was embedded in the U.S. intelligence community for several years following 9/11. His mission was to conduct an organizational assessment and needs analysis, which included over 500 interviews, observational participation, focus groups, and questions. It's an impressive piece of insight.

What he found sounds suspiciously like the state of the insights profession today. He published some of his findings in a book entitled

Analytic Culture in the U.S. Intelligence Community. Read this excerpt and substitute insights for intelligence.

"As it is now practiced, intelligence analysis is art, tradecraft, and science. There are specific tools and techniques to help perform the tasks, but, in the end, it is left to individuals to use their best judgement in making decisions. This is not to say that science is not a part of intelligence analysis. Science is born of organized knowledge, and organizing knowledge requires effort and time. The work on this [project] is intended to help that process by sparking discussion, identifying areas where research exists and ought to be incorporated into the organizational knowledge of intelligence, and identifying areas where not enough research has been performed."

His conclusion is that the intelligence community needs to transform from being craft-focused to being science-oriented. He suggests that the "development of a research agenda for analytic methodology that is focused on collecting effectiveness and validation data is the first step in moving intelligence analysis from a tradecraft model to a scientific model."

His concern with the craft approach is its inefficiency and lack of validation, which should be familiar to all of us. "As long as intelligence analysis continues to be a tradecraft, it will remain a mystery. The quality of the tradecraft depends on the innate cognitive capacities of the individual and the good fortune one has in finding a mentor who has discovered, through many years of trial and error, unique methods that seem to be effective. This process of trial and error is, in general, similar to any scientific process, except that the lessons learned in tradecraft, unlike those of other disciples, often occur without being captured, tested or validated." Sounds hauntingly familiar, doesn't it?

Journey from craft to science

Much has happened in the years since Johnston made the recommendation to move from craft to science. And, indeed, there are some researchers working on effectiveness and validation data today. Dr. David Mandel, often in collaboration with Dr. Philip Tetlock of *Superforecasting* fame and others, is conducting research to help the

intelligence community become increasingly scientific. He has been
a pioneer in the push to assess intelligence analytic processes for years
and has conducted some landmark analyses.

I was fortunate to interview Dr. Mandel and get his perspective on the
progress made, but before we jump ahead to that, we need to better
understand the arc of the intelligence community's journey, because it is
a road that we in the insights industry must travel if we are to survive
and thrive. We should learn from what they have done that works, and
what they have not yet done. To understand their efforts, we need to
start at the beginning.

Roots of intelligence analysis

The roots of a discipline shape what it becomes and how it grows.
Interestingly, for an enterprise twice the size of the insights industry, the
intelligence community is even younger than market research. The roots
of modern-day intelligence analysis can be traced back to World War II
and a Yale historian with a specialization in 19th century French politics
named Sherman Kent.

Just prior to the U.S. joining World War II, Kent was recruited to join
a group of scholars in the newly formed Research & Analysis Branch
(R&A) of the Office of Strategic Services in Washington. In the spirit
of serving the war effort, they called themselves the "Bad Eyes Brigade."
Their purpose was to provide intelligence on foreign countries and
potential theaters of battle. The people best versed in this information
were academics: historians, political scientists, geographers,
anthropologists, economists, and psychologists. The problem was,
no one had ever done this before, and there was no model for how to
do analysis.

There were few in Washington, Kent writes, "who could give any
guidance as to how to go about the business at hand. What intelligence
techniques there were, ready and available, were in their infancy.
Intelligence was to us at that period really nothing in itself; it was, at
best, the sum of what we, from our outside experience, could contribute
to a job to be done."

Kent was pondering how the analysis was to be done because he had a keen interest in methodology. Just prior to joining the intelligence effort he had published *Writing History,* a book that espoused an approach to analysis that emphasized the importance of the scientific method, intellectual plasticity, and deep skepticism of the evidence at hand. The approach was "akin to the method of science which Francis Bacon put forth in the early seventeenth century," he writes.

"It consists of gathering facts...[and] forming hypotheses on the basis of these facts, of testing these hypotheses for traces of one's own ignorance or bias, of cleansing them if possible. The goal of research is to build better hypotheses than already exist and to establish them as relatively more true: it is to reveal a sharp picture of what happened and make a closer approach to actuality than anyone has yet contrived." A colleague later noted, "In many of the passages [of *Writing History*] one need only substitute the words 'intelligence officer' for 'historian.'" Or, indeed, insights analyst.

A unique and interesting aspect of this new endeavor was that it drew upon so many different fields. "Since intelligence required its own methodology, R&A would derive this methodology from several disciplines," writes historian and diplomat Robin Winks. The CIA's Jack Davis says, "One of Kent's legendary achievements was to talk reluctant economists into serving under the direction of a historian."

Following the war, the department was broken up and Kent served in the State Department for a time before returning to Yale. Having developed a taste for intelligence analysis, he wrote *Strategic Intelligence for American World Policy.* It was well received in and out of government and became the blueprint for how intelligence analysis was done. When Harry Truman set up the Central Intelligence Agency, Kent was asked to lead its Office of National Estimates (ONE). There he shaped the future of analysis in the intelligence community, in the U.S. and abroad.

As academic and author J. Peter Sclobic writes, "When Kent joined the Research and Analysis Branch, U.S. intelligence analysis was a haphazard affair. By the time he left the CIA, it was an orderly process staffed by career analysts who hewed to a strict methodology that prioritized objectivity in the face of ambiguity and neutrality in the face of ideology. Kent's insistence on disinterested analysis gave ONE a degree of independence from Washington politics, and his reverence for the scientific method legitimized its work on prediction."

Kent was insistent on questioning assumptions and biases and favored generating multiple hypotheses, but he did not prescribe a specific set of rules or exact methods for extracting insights from information. As much as his methodology was "akin" to science, it was not science per se.

The next generation took a step closer. Enter CIA methodologist Richards J. Heuer Jr., whose hugely influential *The Psychology of Intelligence Analysis* helped propel the intelligence community toward a more scientific approach to analysis.

Into the psychology of intelligence analysis

Richards "Dick" Heuer, a philosophy student, was recruited out of university to join the CIA. He worked in operations, which sounds kind of dull. But here is how the CIA describes the role of an operations officer on the careers page of its website: "you will focus on clandestinely spotting, assessing, developing, recruiting, and handling non-US citizens with access to foreign intelligence vital to US foreign policy and national security decisionmakers. You will be expected to build relationships based on rapport and trust using sound judgment, integrity, and the ability to assess character and motivation." In other words, Dick Heuer spent 24 years as a spy. Then he moved on to methodology.

Heuer describes it this way: "In 1975 I arranged to shift from the operations side of CIA to the analysis side in order to work in a new Analytic Methodology Division that had recently been created in direct response to criticism by prominent academics that the agency's analytic methods were way out of date. Our task was to examine quantitative methods that were developed in the 1960s during what was called the behavioral revolution in academic political science, and to test how these methods could be applied to intelligence analysis." Then, at the 1977 International Studies Association (ISA) conference, he chaired a panel entitled "Quantitative Approaches to Political Intelligence: The CIA Experience." There he met an Israeli officer who was tasked with the same challenge of improving intelligence analysis methodology in his country.

"Immediately after that ISA presentation, I was approached by a man with a foreign accent who said, 'Vee need to talk. Zee answer ees not in zee numbers, it's in zee head,'" Heuer recounts. "That sounded interesting, so we had lunch, and he told me about Kahneman and Tversky's path-breaking work in cognitive psychology."

"I then read Kahneman and Tversky's work, and that was the beginning of my continuing interest in cognitive psychology. I then began writing a series of papers and lecturing to CIA training courses on the cognitive problems and to a lesser extent the group process and organizational problems one encounters in doing analysis. One of the lessons I learned during that period is still very applicable today. If you want to change how analysis is done, you need to show analysts how you can help them. I could do that after my research in cognitive psychology taught me about how the mind works."

In *Psychology of Intelligence Analysis* he collected together the learnings from these papers and lectures. The essence of his premise is that "Intelligence analysts should be self-conscious about their reasoning processes. They should think about how they make judgements and reach conclusions, not just about the judgements and conclusions themselves."

In a foreword to the book, former CIA Deputy Director of Intelligence Douglas MacEachin sums up Heuer's position this way: "Dick Heuer makes it clear that the pitfalls the human mental process sets for analysts cannot be eliminated; they are part of us. What can be done is to train people how to look for and recognize these mental obstacles, and how to develop procedures designed to offset them."

Heuer, the former philosophy student, opens the book with a section about "thinking about thinking" before reviewing various perceptual and cognitive biases from the literature. He builds on Kent's encouragement to consider multiple hypotheses and to be skeptical, and caps the book off with a description of a technique he devised to encourage a more scientific and systematic approach to the consideration of alternative hypotheses.

ACH—a structured analytic technique

Heuer devised a technique called Analysis of Competing Hypotheses, known as ACH. It's a fascinating approach to coming to an insight. It forces people to look beyond the data and to consider why things are as they are. And, cognizant of our biases, it attempts to make us grapple with our cognitive limitations.

ACH also encourages people to step outside their own perspectives and connect with others in the journey to insight. It chronicles people's thinking and the steps they took—so that others can retrace those steps and see how conclusions were arrived at.

Heuer lays out his process in eight steps. Each step is more like a guideline than a specific, prescribed process. This makes the use of ACH more accessible and open to interpretation. But this variability also has the effect of making it difficult to measure the effectiveness of using ACH. Nonetheless, ACH provides great food for thought when thinking about how we get to an insight.

Here is Heuer's "Step by Step Outline of the Analysis of Competing Hypotheses."

"1. Identify the possible hypotheses to be considered. Use a group of analysts with different perspectives to brainstorm the possibilities.

2. Make a list of significant evidence and arguments for and against each hypothesis.

3. Prepare a matrix of hypotheses across the top and evidence down the side. Analyze the 'diagnosticity' of the evidence and arguments—that is, identify which items are most helpful in judging the relative likelihood of the hypotheses.

4. Refine the matrix. Reconsider the hypotheses and delete evidence and arguments that have no diagnostic value.

5. Draw tentative conclusions about the relative likelihood of each hypothesis. Proceed by trying to disprove the hypotheses rather than prove them.

6. Analyze how sensitive your conclusion is to a few critical items of evidence. Consider the consequences for your analysis if that evidence were wrong, misleading, or subject to a different interpretation.

7. Report conclusions. Discuss the relative likelihood of all hypotheses, not just the most likely one.

8. Identify milestones for future observation that may indicate events are taking a different course than expected."

Learning from ACH

The worlds of intelligence analysis and insights are similar, but not the same. So, the approach of ACH is not a direct fit with the process of generating an insight, but there is much to be learned from its example. "A principal advantage of the analysis of competing hypotheses is that it forces you to give a fairer shake to all the alternatives," Heuer states.

Let's start with the first point. "Identify the possible hypotheses to be considered. Use a group of analysts with different perspectives to brainstorm the possibilities." These are two important strategies that are useful for insights professionals. We tend to try to leap straight to a conclusion, without trying to consider other possible explanations.

This first step enjoins us to think about multiple alternative explanations—not just the first one that "makes sense" and can be supported by some evidence. The second important aspect of this first step is working not in isolation, but in a group—and not just a group of like-minded souls, but a diverse group.

Heuer explains why this way: "Psychological research into how people go about generating hypotheses shows that people are actually rather poor at thinking of all the possibilities. If a person does not even generate the right hypothesis for consideration, obviously he or she will not get the correct answer."

Heuer suggests, "At this early hypothesis generation stage, it is very useful to bring together a group of analysts with different backgrounds and perspectives. Brainstorming in a group stimulates the imagination and may bring out possibilities that individual members of the group had not thought of."

This can sound like such a challenge and effort that it's easy to dismiss it as impractical for the insights industry. But think of it this way: what's to stop you from picking up a box of donuts, grabbing people from a couple of different departments, and brainstorming for 15 minutes?

What if you could grab the new person in sales, the old guy from sales promotions, the person who has been project managing the brand tracker, and the guy who used to work on the brand but now has a different job in marketing? How much broader would your perspective be?

Starting by stepping back and getting outside input is a "stitch in time saves nine" move. By starting broad you can avoid getting sucked into tunnel vision. By obtaining multiple perspectives you have the potential to dodge the confirmation bias that you would be unable to see in yourself.

The case for and against hypotheses

Heuer's second step, "Make a list of significant evidence and arguments for and against each hypothesis," is helpful in that it compels us to seek out multiple pieces of information that both support and refute these ideas. This forces us to not just accept a single piece of data that supports our conjecture. It requires us to think more broadly and to consider both sides of the argument.

"For each hypothesis, ask yourself this question: If this hypothesis is true, what should I expect to be seeing or not seeing?" Heuer suggests. Crucially, he also points out the need to "Note the absence of evidence as well as its presence." This, he says, "recalls the Sherlock Holmes story in which the vital clue was that the dog did not bark in the night. One's attention tends to focus on what is reported rather than what is not reported. It requires a conscious effort to think about what is missing but should be present if a given hypothesis were true."

Let's say we want to know what drives a buying decision, so that the organization understands how to best invest funds to get maximum sales. We've done a driver analysis, where we have focused on brand image. The model only partially explains why people buy, but the marketing team loves it because it lets them lobby for funds to support advertising. But you know that you are missing most of the reason why people buy. If one of the hypotheses we are testing is that brand is an important driver of sales and therefore worthy of investment, we must look at what evidence we have that both supports and refutes the hypothesis.

The driver analysis gives us evidence that brand does influence purchasing. But it also gives us evidence that something else explains the majority of why people buy. What if we dive into the data and look at the brand's image and we find out the brand is basically undifferentiated from the others? Yes, we see a relationship between brand image and buying—because purchasers like the brand better and associate it with more good things, while non-buyers don't. But does that prove causality? Is brand image the chicken or the egg? Which came first?

What if positive brand image arises from experience with the product? And experience with the product was stimulated by a point of sale promotion? That means we should probably look for that old report on the impact of point of sales promotions that got mentioned in the brainstorming phase and add that to the evidence. And think about what else might be going on that is driving sales, other than brand. What if we see from brand tracking that brand image has gotten stronger, but sales have remained flat? Is there a question that we did not ask that holds the answer?

Enter the matrix

The third step of ACH asks people to "prepare a matrix with hypotheses across the top and evidence down the side." This has two important effects. One is that by writing down our hypotheses we must commit to a concise version of our ideas. The second is that by summarizing the evidence in a way that fits on the grid we are required to focus on the forest and not the trees.

The next part of this step is to look at each point of evidence (the rows in our grid) and determine whether it helps us determine which hypothesis is likely to be correct. Basically, does it contribute any unique and differentiating information? Heuer calls this analyzing the "diagnosticity" of the evidence.

"Diagnosticity," he suggests, "may be illustrated by a medical analogy. A high-temperature reading may have great value in telling a doctor that a patient is sick, but relatively little in determining which illness a person is suffering from. Because a high temperature is consistent with so many hypotheses about a patient's illness, this evidence has limited diagnostic value in determining which illness (hypothesis) is the more likely one."

The fourth step in ACH is to refine the matrix by weeding out information that does not help support or disprove a hypothesis, and then setting aside that evidence in a second list that records what information was considered.

Let's say we looked at Net Promotor Scores (NPS), which have been stable for some time. They don't particularly prove or disprove that marketing is driving sales or any of our other hypotheses. So, we set NPS aside, noting that we put it on the shelf.

Prove it—or not

Step five is stress testing each hypothesis by trying to disprove it. Here Heuer looks to the scientific method for inspiration.

"In evaluating the relative likelihood of alternative hypotheses, start by looking for evidence or logical deductions that enable you to reject hypotheses, or at least determine that they are unlikely. A fundamental precept of the scientific method is to proceed by rejecting or eliminating hypotheses, while tentatively accepting only those hypotheses that cannot be refuted. The scientific method obviously cannot be applied *in toto* to intuitive judgement, but the principle of seeking to disprove hypotheses, rather than confirm them, is useful."

Resilient or easily shattered?

Step six enjoins you to "Analyze how sensitive your conclusion is to a few critical items of evidence. Consider the consequences for your analysis if that evidence were wrong, misleading, or subject to a different interpretation."

Let's say you have the hypothesis that point of sale promotions are driving product selection. If your main support for that hypothesis is some intriguing in-store ethnography that was done in Seattle, then step six suggests you might want to search out other evidence—or at least be aware of the risk of making a decision based on a single point of observation. The insights coming from that research might be rich and revealing, but they may not be what you want to bet the farm on.

"When analysis turns out to be wrong," Heuer says, "it is often because of key assumptions that went unchallenged and proved invalid. It is a truism that analysts should identify and question assumptions, but this is much easier said than done. The problem is to determine which assumptions merit questioning. One advantage of the ACH procedure is that it tells you what needs to be rechecked."

Make the call, but keep an open mind and follow through

"Report conclusions" is where step seven lays it on the line and makes the call. But Heuer cautions analysts to "discuss the relative likelihood of all hypotheses, not just the most likely one."

"Decisionmakers need to make decisions on the basis of a full set of alternative possibilities, not just the single most likely alternative. Contingency of fallback plans may be needed in case one of the less likely alternatives turns out to be true."

The final step is a good one, because it highlights the value of following up on whether we made the right call, so we can course correct if we got it wrong or if the market dynamics are changing.

Step eight is to "Identify milestones for future observation that may indicate events are taking a different course than expected."

Let's say the conclusion is that marketing is driving sales. But the brand tracker suggests that while brand image is becoming significantly more positive, sales are flat. That should trigger monitoring of the situation and re-evaluation of the relationship of brand to sales as new data emerges.

"Analytical conclusions should always be regarded as tentative," Heuer cautions. "The situation may change, or it may remain unchanged while you receive new information that alters your appraisal."

This is but one of the structured analytic techniques (SAT) Heuer and others devised, but it is the most influential and the most enduring.

This look at the approach of the CIA and the forces that pushed them toward adopting a more rigorous and consistent approach to analysis is instructive. The world of insights needs to move away from approaching problems in isolation, ignorant of our biases and with a tendency to embrace the easy solution and get sucked into tunnel vision.

The approaches of Kent and Heuer are inspiring and suggest some strategies that insights could learn from. And while ACH may be a bit involved for a small tactical decision, it makes a great deal of sense when tackling bigger questions like informing resource allocation.

But a key question remains: is there proof it is effective?

Chapter 9: Trudging toward science

"Science, like intelligence, can be messy. Progress is slow and only comes from efforts to push boundaries."
Welton Chang, Elissabeth Berdini, David R. Mandel & Philip E. Tetlock,

Are structured analytic techniques such as the Analysis of Competing Hypotheses (ACH) a magic bullet? Do we just create an equivalent for the insights industry and instantly eliminate cognitive bias? In a word, no.

ACH and other structured analytic techniques are a waystation in the journey from craft to science. Kent started the journey by encouraging rigor and science-based reasoning. Heuer furthered it by pointing out problems with bias and attempting to impose some structure on analysis. But the next step is assessing the effectiveness of these techniques, and continually making improvements based on the assessments. Only then can intelligence analysis become more of a science. That's precisely what decision scientists like David Mandel, Philip Tetlock, and others are urging the intelligence community to do.

They are at the forefront of a movement calling for the intelligence community to question their techniques, understand the effects of them, and, ultimately, improve decision making. Their story reminds us that we should not simply accept approaches to analysis that seem to make sense and appear beneficial. It is not enough to think about thinking. Their example reveals the importance of applying the rigors of science by testing the effect of analytic strategies.

Despite relatively widespread use, ACH has been the subject of little research. The studies that have been conducted are not terribly encouraging. But learnings from the world of decision sciences point to promising paths forward.

Better together

In the 1970s and 1980s, commercials for Reese's Peanut Butter Cups featured situations in which two people, one eating peanut butter and one eating chocolate, collided. One person would exclaim, "You got your peanut butter on my chocolate!" and the other would cry out, "You got your chocolate in my peanut butter!" Then they'd taste the mixture, be delighted, and shout out, "Two great tastes that taste great together!" The collision of decision science and intelligence analysis has one of its own chocolate and peanut butter moments.

David Mandel is a cognitive and social psychologist with a longstanding interest in judgment and decision-making research. Alan Barnes was an intelligence analyst and manager of analysts in the Canadian intelligence community for over 25 years, with many of those years as Director of the Middle East and Africa Division in the Intelligence Assessment Secretariat.

Keenly aware of the effects of intelligence failures, Barnes was motivated to ensure the analysis of his team was accurate and communicated clearly, and he believed measurement and feedback would help. He had started to gather data on his analysts' effectiveness when he met David Mandel, who, after several years in academia, had recently joined the Department of National Defence.

"He described to me the policies that he had implemented and the data he was collecting," Dr Mandel explained to me. "When I met him, I said, 'Oh, you basically set up conditions for running a forecasting skill verification study,' which was his intent. He wanted to be able to keep track of the accuracy of his analysts."

Mandel said, "I was able to describe to him some of the statistical methods that we could use that would go beyond the kind of rudimentary analysis he was calculating at the time. So that's where our partnership got forged. As a result of forging that partnership, we also tightened up the methodology for collecting and keeping track of the data."

"It was a fortuitous meeting. I met him just at the time that he was engaged in this activity, and I happened to be a behavioral scientist with the right set of skills to be able to do the analysis on this project. You don't always find that in government. Of course, intelligence directors don't usually meet with scientists."

"I found it fascinating and, aside from the forecasting study that I worked on with Alan, I realized that this was a community of experts who were basically in the business of making judgements, and their judgements had to be communicated clearly to other people who were in the business of making decisions. Really weighty decisions for their country. Decisions about national security, decisions about how to promote the prosperity of their country."

"I found it interesting, given that I've had a longstanding interest in judgment and decision making. And this brought me into an expert community that I quickly realized did not have a lot of scientific validation of the methods and standards that they had implemented."

Mandel and Barnes analyzed over 1,500 forecasts coming from over six years of Barnes's department's output. They reported, "Our findings warrant tempered optimism about the quality of strategic intelligence forecasts. The forecasts fared exceptionally well in terms of discrimination and calibration…. The results provide a stark contrast with Tetlock's findings [on expert political judgement]. Whereas the best political forecasters in his sample explained about 20% of the outcome variance, forecasts in this study explained 76% of the variance in geopolitical outcomes."

Putting ACH to the test

These positive findings attracted the attention of the international intelligence community and led Mandel to further work with intelligence analysts and analytic techniques. Mandel collaborated with Mandeep Dhami of Middlesex University and Ian Belton of the University of Strathclyde in Glasgow on one of the few studies on "The 'analysis of competing hypotheses' in intelligence analysis." They found, "There was mixed evidence for ACH's ability to reduce confirmation bias, and we observed that ACH may increase judgement inconsistency and error." Much of Heuer's efforts with SATs focused on making people aware of biases—which is a necessary first step. But, as Mandel points out, awareness is not enough. "This is one of the key points that Kahneman and Tversky made in their work on heuristics and biases. It's not enough to know that you're biased. Just knowing that you're biased doesn't enable you to correct the bias. In fact, there's another bias, a meta bias that [Princeton psychology professor] Emily Pronin and others have worked on called the bias blind spot. The idea is that we're blind to the fact that these cognitive biases affect us. We're much more able to see that they affect other people. So, we can see the biases in other people, but we think we're immune from them. And that, of course, makes it harder to learn when we actually are susceptible to them."

About his testing of ACH, Mandel explains, "there is some evidence that ACH doesn't really help judgment accuracy at all. It doesn't seem to harm it. But it does seem to actually have a detrimental effect on the logical coherence of analyst judgment.

"Like if I ask you what's the probability of it raining today and you say, 'Well I think there's a 30% chance.' And then I ask you a minute later what's the chance of it not raining and you say, '90% chance'; it doesn't add up, right? It either is going to rain or it isn't. So, for binary events, the probability should add up to 100%. We found that analysts who used ACH were more prone to violating those kinds of axioms than analysts who were just left to their own devices...."

But why is this so hard?

Mandel teamed up with University of Pennsylvania professor and author Philip Tetlock and fellow decision scientists Welton Chang and Elissabeth Berdini to author a paper entitled "Restructuring structured analytic techniques in intelligence." In it they unpack some theories as to why SATs seem to fail to deliver on their promise.

"We propose that the root problems with SATs derive from the failure to deploy best practices in coping with the two fundamental sources of error that bedevil all efforts to improve human judgment: systematic bias and random noise in the processes by which people generate, test and update their hunches about the world."

They identify two key problems with SATs. One is that they tend to treat biases as working only one way. They note that "well-intentioned attempts to reduce one bias, say, over-confidence, will amplify its opposing bias, under-confidence." This is an issue with ACH, for example.

The other problem is that, in multi-stage assessments, there can be cumulative error which goes undetected. SATs lack checks and balances to combat the reality that "the noise in the conclusions from the one stage gets fed into the next," which is a problem they call "noise neglect."

The authors have some good points. While it seems logical to combat confirmation bias with critical thinking, we must acknowledge the fact that biases cut both ways. We need to consider both the positive and the negative effects. Is critical thinking potentially leading us toward problems like under-confidence in our conclusions?

The question of "noise neglect" is particularly germane for the world of insights. Now that people are moving more toward multi-stage and iterative investigations, we do need to be aware that conclusions we make early on can blind us to other possibilities later. Thus, "noise neglect" can lead to tunnel vision. We need to keep our minds open, even if prior studies suggest we're on the right path.

"Both problems," Chang, Berdini, Tetlock and Mandel write, "stem from the lack of sustained efforts to subject SATs to scientific tests of efficacy and scrutinizing the processes for logical validity. The net result is that it is difficult to know when SATs are sparing us from serious mistakes, when they are creating more problems than they are solving, or when they are just ineffective."

Show me the way to go home

So, this is fun. We become conscious that we are biased, but the techniques designed to deter bias may not help, and they might even hinder. What's an insights professional to do?

Is it time to throw up our hands, suggest analysis is a subjective art and that all explanations are equally valid? That might work if you were a tenured professor with a proclivity for postmodernism. But, in most organizations, that's not an option. Our clients need insights that will uncover new opportunities and shape decision-making. They can't just accept random interpretations colored by bias. They need insights they can make profitable decisions on.

The methods of the insights industry have their roots in social research and psychometrics that date back a century or more. Our techniques have changed relatively little since then. Little work has been done to validate or update these methods—let alone prove their value. We need to heed the advice of Mandel and Tetlock and look to best practices outside the world of insights. And we must test our methods and not just assume they are optimal because they seem to work.

"The IC needs a diverse infusion of ideas from scientists outside the IC," suggest Mandel and Tetlock. "It needs those scientists not only to put forward their best ideas, but also to test them in rigorous experiments or experimental tournaments. The IC should take the most promising results and work with scientific teams to transition the ideas into analytic processes. Those teams should also work with their IC counterparts to devise rigorous ways of trialing those processes, and the results of those trials should be taken seriously. ...[and] reasons for variance in efficacy should be examined. Is the original idea doomed to transition failure, or was the transition strategy flawed but correctable?"

Does that sound to you like something the insights industry should do? It does to me.

Forecasting our future

Tetlock is famous for his work on forecasting, and his use of tournaments to identify the characteristics of good forecasters. He is perhaps best known for being able to prove conclusively that, when it comes to predicting the future, "the average expert was roughly as accurate as a dart throwing chimpanzee."

His ambitious Good Judgement Program has been increasingly able to identify what makes for a good forecaster. One tournament the Good Judgement Program team participated in, which ran from 2011 to 2013, was sponsored by the U.S. government's Intelligence Advanced Research Projects Activity (IARPA). It involved over 150,000 forecasts for 199 events made by 743 people.

In a paper summarizing the findings, Tetlock, Barbara Mellers, and others conclude that the best forecasters "were better at inductive reasoning, pattern detection, cognitive flexibility, and open-mindedness. They had greater understanding of geopolitics, training in probabilistic reasoning, and opportunities to succeed in cognitively enriched team environments."

Building on this learning, and others, Tetlock, Mandel, Berdini, and Chang make suggestions for restructuring structured analytic techniques. First and foremost, they call for standardized testing of SATs to determine their effectiveness and establishing a feedback loop to continuously improve them. They propose SATs be modified to incorporate probability theory. The aim of this inclusion is not only to improve the forecasts, but also to be able to track their accuracy and provide feedback to analysts. And they suggest analyzing test-retest reliability of forecasts to measure the effectiveness of efforts to debias and reduce noise.

Insights are not the same as forecasts. They are less amenable to being nailed down quite so concretely. But we do have an outcome measure that is vital to our organizations and key to protecting and expanding our budgets: the return on investments from our insights. The Global Research Business Network has been leading the way in championing a focus on ROI in the insights industry, working with the Boston Consulting Group to outline how insights departments can become more ROI-focused. Their business impact initiative includes handbooks on measuring and improving ROI from insights.

But ROI can't be the only measure of impact, Greg Dinsmore, Director of Media Insights at Rogers Communications, told me, "I think insights are highly valuable, but it is very, very difficult to decide on what the exact value is. And when people are figuring out budgets, it's tricky to assign direct value to insights." Part of the problem, he explains, is that "There is a disconnect in the way people justify insights versus the way that they actually should be justified. I think people justify insights with the idea it will help them make good decisions. And I think that's true to a point. But I think there is even greater value in research stopping you from making bad decisions. That, to me, is a higher payoff. But it's really hard to show."

Ciara O'Connell, Senior Director, Consumer & Customer Insights, Campbell Snacks at Campbell Soup Company, is also conscious of making sure the insights her team generates are measurably moving the business forward. "We're always looking to not just drive insights, but to put insights into action. The challenging part is, 'what is that action resulting in?'" She notes the effects of insights may not show up right away.

"If you're developing a more effective campaign, if you're working on updated packaging, or whatever it is, when you report on the year's results, the impact is not always immediately evident. It can be the next year before you are able to prove out the results. That is a consistent challenge of ours, especially when we're compared to other groups who might see more immediate return."

Despite these challenges, she still feels it is essential to strive to show ROI. "I continue to encourage my team to say, 'Look at the work you did. What were the outcomes? What were the measurable results?' There is no perfect process other than to say, 'Guys, we've got to get better at this—proving the value of our work.'"

Researcher, evaluate thyself

While proving ROI has its challenges, the proposals made by Mandel, Tetlock, and others suggests we must find a way to draw linkages between ways of formalizing and testing analytic practices and ROI. That would help us improve our craft and ensure we have the budgets needed to thrive. In an environment where information is everywhere, evidence that insights drive ROI is scare.

We need to strive to develop a more rigorous approach to analysis that is cognizant of biases and noise. There is every reason for us to focus on educating researchers on analogical reasoning, pattern detection, flexible reasoning, and probabilistic thinking. And we must consider how we can make more use of teams, and have those teams focused on sharing ideas and debating rationales.

This notion of teamwork is an important one and is a strategy used by many other types of sense-makers to detect bias and expose blind spots, as we shall see.

Chapter 10: Battling bias

"Don't believe everything you think."
Bumper sticker

One way the intelligence community has tried to grapple with bias is by using structured analytic techniques. But there is no proof those methods work—hence Mandel, Tetlok, and others calling for a more rigorous approach to the design and testing of strategies to work around the problem of bias.

Some say it's impossible to defeat bias, suggesting it is so hardwired into our consciousness that we are unable to get past it. We know other people are biased, but we can't see it in ourselves.

"Bias is paradoxical," writes Tom James in *The Atlantic*. "It can drive people's actions one way, while their conscious minds strain in the opposite direction. It can be a feeling people hardly notice, but one that can profoundly change how they see the world. And it's fairly straightforward to explain, but difficult to accept."

What's difficult to accept is the fact that what we perceive as reality is in fact a thin representation, conjured up out of very sparse data. It is not easy to come to terms with the truth that our rational thinking is mainly used to generate plausible reasons for why we do things for reasons we are not conscious of. We know we have biases, but we can't see them, just like we can't see the literal blind spot in our vision.

"To paraphrase Mark Twain's observation about the weather, everyone talks about the peril of cognitive biases, but no one ever does anything about it," says the CIA's Jack Davis.

But that doesn't stop people from trying. All sorts of sense-makers see the very real effects of biases and are attempting to counter them.

Some are doing so in rigorous ways. But even those doing research on the effects of debiasing strategies admit the road ahead is long.

In a review of studies on cognitive bias in medical diagnosis, Dr. Mark Graber and his colleagues admit, "The field is immature and progress in reducing diagnostic error will require considerable research to evaluate the relative merits of these different ideas, refinements in the methodology of defining and measuring outcomes in preventing diagnostic error and harm, and leveraging advances in other aspects of medical decision-making and cognitive sciences that may make medical diagnosis more reliable."

If this confirms your belief that the problem of bias is intractable, you can skip this chapter. If you are open to a competing hypothesis, read on.

The problem is real

Bias kills. It is estimated that medical errors cause "100,000 unnecessary deaths" and "perhaps one million excess injuries" each year in the U.S. alone. One meta-analysis of investigations into the link between cognitive bias and misdiagnosis found cognitive bias to be implicated in, depending upon which study you looked at, between 37% and 77% of cases.

With so much at stake, it is comforting to know there are researchers in medicine seeking to find ways to combat biases in diagnosis and treatment. Similar work is occurring in the world of justice, where the number of wrongfully convicted continues to grow, revealing the extent to which bias can lead to outcomes that nobody wants.

By better understanding the role bias plays, the justice system has been able to move away from an unhelpful blame game and toward a more hopeful focus on achieving just outcomes. "Traditionally, prosecutorial decision making has been studied through a lens of fault, blame, and intentional wrongdoing," writes law professor Alafair Burke. "Consistent with this lens, those who have studied the downsides of broad prosecutorial discretion have blamed bad prosecutorial decisions on overzealousness, flawed cultural and individual values, and a lack of moral courage."

The problem is, the evidence doesn't really support this. A simple story of malevolent prosecutors seeking convictions at any cost is attractive, because it follows a simple script of bad versus good, but the reality is more complex.

Burke is encouraged that a "growing literature seeks to attribute poor prosecutorial decision making to a set of information-processing biases that we all share, rather than exclusively to ethical or moral lapses. From this perspective, prosecutorial resistance to defense claims of innocence can be viewed as deep (and inherently human) adherences to the 'sticky' presumptions of guilt that result from various forms of cognitive bias that can impede the neutrality of prosecutors throughout their handling of a case."

Having correctly identified the problem, it becomes possible to work toward solving it. In the insights industry we are not as advanced in combating bias as our fellow sense-makers in medicine or the law. There is much we can learn from the solutions that these disciplines, and others, have investigated.

The first step

The first step in the journey to confronting bias is creating awareness and admitting it is a problem. It is like step one in a twelve step addictions program. I'll start: "My name is Andrew and I have a problem with bias. All my analyses—including this one—are affected by my biases."

Just making people aware of bias does not help them confront it. Education is necessary, but not sufficient. As Edinburgh-based physicians E.D. O'Sullivan and S.J. Schofield write, "while focused educational sessions seem an intuitive and practical approach to mitigating bias, the evidence to support this is mixed and there are certainly enough negative studies to suggest it would be a low-yield intervention at best."

Burke confirms this is the case in the law as well: "commentators have continually called for increased prosecutorial training regarding the dangers of cognitive bias…. Unfortunately, the empirical evidence also suggests that cognitive bias is stubborn, and that education is an unlikely panacea."

Basic education won't change the situation. But education in the form of specific feedback on past decisions has been shown to be effective in reducing bias. "A systematic review of feedback across all medical areas (not solely diagnosis) concluded that feedback improves performance in selected settings, especially if the feedback is intensive," Graber et al. report in their paper "Cognitive interventions to reduce diagnostic error: a narrative review."

"Feedback also offers the potential to reduce errors by helping develop expertise," they explain. "Feedback is also the key to reducing overconfidence, which in turn could open the door for clinicians to appreciate the possibility of their own errors and take actions to avoid them."

Teamwork, doubt, and structured techniques, including checklists, also hold promise as strategies for fighting bias.

Chapter 11: Teamwork works

"I get by with a little help from my friends."
Paul McCartney and John Lennon

"When you are making important decisions and you want to get it right, you should get the help of your friends," Daniel Kahneman advises. "And you should get the help of a friend who doesn't take you too seriously, since they're not too impressed by your biases." This use of friends to expose bias is one of many ways of drawing on the power of teams.

In the worlds of the social and hard sciences, peer review is a common mechanism for catching error in general, and bias in particular. It is one example of how teamwork can identify and neutralize bias. The idea of peer review is not new. It appears in the 9th century Arab physician and ethicist Ishāq ibn ʿAlī al-Ruhāwī's *Ethics for the Physician*. In this work he describes a method by which duplicate notes on a patient's case are to be kept so that they can be reviewed by a local council of physicians, to determine if standards of medical care are being met.

"Second opinions and consultations bring fresh eyes to examine a case, a powerful and effective way to find and correct diagnostic errors," concludes Graber et al.'s paper. Medical rounds, in which patients' cases are reviewed and discussed by medical teams, serve as a tool for education, provide directed feedback, are a source of alternative ideas, and offer a check on blind spots. Many hospital-based physicians start each day with rounds. How much less biased and richer might our insights be if, each week, we started with a multi-disciplinary team commenting on our analysis?

Law professor Burke sees a second opinion as a safeguard against the kinds of bias that can lead to wrongful convictions. She suggests, "A 'fresh look' by attorneys unassociated with initial sticky charging decisions may dilute the biasing effects of selective information processing and belief perseverance." "A fresh-look attorney would also be in a better position to bring neutrality to a defendant's claim of innocence," she believes, "because she would have less of a stake in avoiding the cognitive dissonance of having charged or convicted an innocent person."

Watching video as a team sport

Our NYPD detective uses video a great deal because it provides concrete evidence—the kind that appeals to prosecutors and juries— and avoids the vagaries of eyewitness accounts. He told me, "They want to see the incident on video. They want to see the perp on video. They want everything on video. So, a tremendous amount of what I do now is just pulling video from places. Just surveillance video, what have you. People's cell phone videos, people's pictures. I work in Manhattan, so there's video cameras everywhere.

"This case I'm working now, it's a carjacking. I have these guys before the incident walking down 29th Street towards where they steal this car. So, now I just go back and check the video. 'Okay, they're walking eastbound down 29th. Now I have them crossing 2nd. Now I have them crossing 3rd.' So, I work backwards, the opposite direction that they went.

"I tracked them as far as 7th Avenue, and I'm down here on the west side now, because they ditched this car on 26th Street. Then [the perpetrator] walks around three blocks circuitously and ducks into the shelter where he lives.

"So, now I'll need to fight it out with this shelter and my department's legal team to try to get someone to tell me who came in at 1:15 that night, because it's obviously my guy who did this carjacking, because I followed him from 16 different cameras as he walked around Chelsea here and then into this shelter."

But this detective doesn't just watch the video alone. He asks others to watch too, because he is self-aware he'll be blind to things and not know it. He explains, "The best thing I've done is have somebody else watch it with me. I have these two other guys on my team. My two immediate bosses are great. They're wonderful, lot of experience, very smart guys. We upload all these videos into our case files so people can watch them. People will review them and just email you and be like 'Hey I reviewed your video, and it looks like the guy has a hand tattoo. I don't know if you saw that.' Just strange stuff you wouldn't think of. So, a lot of people watch these cases. The bigger the case, the more people get involved." In the case of this carjacking, he put extra effort into it because the victim was "really badly hurt."

"It's really helpful because they're seeing it fresh," he says. "If they don't know much about your case, they don't walk into it looking for what you've already seen. They see it on their own. They end up seeing more stuff, just other people, other involvement, or interpreting things in a way that you wouldn't."

It's all part of the process

Having one's analysis commented on by others is baked into the intelligence community's process. "When your work begins to gel into something concrete, then [peer feedback] becomes a much more formal structure, and that has both a horizontal and a vertical aspect to it," a former CIA analyst and current professor of intelligence analysis told me. "The horizontal part of it, before something goes to senior policymakers, is that it has to make its circuit around. Especially if you're getting a little bit outside of your lane. So, if I would do something about a problem and it would have a heavy diplomatic angle to it, I would have to send it over to somebody at the State Department for them to do a sanity check on it. And certainly, if the issue was whether to deploy troops and military kinds of things, then it would have to go over to the Pentagon."

The input from people with different sources of expertise is important because it helps people shake free of what can quickly become shared assumptions and group blind spots. Mark Noll was Notre Dame University's Francis A. McAnaney Professor of History. As an historian, he is acutely aware of how bias can cloud people's perceptions and how peer review can be a tonic.

Noll feels that "a community of criticism, a community of colleagues who aren't afraid to say, 'You've got it wrong here,' is really important. Ideally the peer review process will be a check against presumptive interpretation of the meaning of the research. And I think it mostly works. But no process is flawless." He is concerned that if you don't obtain feedback from a diverse set of sources, the value of your work is limited. He sees that happening in the academic sphere when there is hyper-specialization. He says peer review works "Only if there hasn't been a kind of breaking off into hermetically sealed silos of reinforcement." In such situations people's points of view can become too homogeneous and "you lose the advantage of having more critical voices."

Intelligence Analysis for Tomorrow: Advances from the Behavioral and Social Sciences is a report commissioned by the National Research Council. It notes, "When people with heterogeneous backgrounds work together, their perspectives emerge in different ways, allowing more knowledge and solutions to emerge. Diversity can be sought in subject-matter expertise, functional background, personal experience and mission perspective. Such sharing allows analyses to be richer and deeper, with better understood strengths and weaknesses, whereas individuals working in isolation are more limited by their assumptions and myopic about the limits of their knowledge. Simply communicating one's assumptions, which is more likely when team members of different backgrounds collaborate, can expose gaps in logic and information. Exposure to contrasting perspectives can reveal errors and promote re-conceptualization."

Teamwork time

For the insights industry, the traditional model of researchers working in relative isolation creates a breeding ground for bias. External suppliers tend to get exposure mostly to their clients, who are internal researchers. Internal researchers tend to connect with a single stakeholder that represents just one slice of the business. We need a broader approach whereby preliminary insights get a reality check from people outside research or marketing. Feedback from sales, regulatory, customer service, government relations, or whoever is relevant can expose our blind spots.

Have you ever been in the uncomfortable situation of triumphantly revealing your brilliant insights and recommendations at a presentation only to have operations or sales point out a gaping hole in your thinking? I have, and it's not fun. Why did it happen? Because I viewed the problem through a research and marketing lens, and I was unaware of other people's perspectives. That's a problem that broad consultation and the solicitation of feedback, before the presentation, can readily solve.

Obviously not all projects need a village. There are practical considerations as well. In *Intelligence Analysis for Tomorrow* the authors suggest, "Because IC entities, like all organizations, operate in a resource-constrained environment, the costs of collaboration can outweigh its benefits. A good rule of thumb is a 'law of requisite variety': a group's heterogeneity should match the complexity of the problems it is tasked to solve. With heterogeneous teams, process loss can outweigh the benefits of collaboration for simple problems, with the balance shifting for complex problems." Or, as the NYPD detective puts it, "the bigger the case, the more people get involved."

Southwest Airlines finds great value in having multiple perspectives, so the analysts have regular meetings to review and comment on each other's work. "We meet together as a team and share insight development across teams," Paul Sacco, Director, Customer Intelligence, told me. "We offer up what people haven't thought of. We keep asking, 'have we thought of all the angles on this?'"

Greg Dinsmore of Rogers Communications invests heavily in peer feedback. His group of analysts devotes a three-hour session each week to review and solicit feedback on what people are working on. The basic theme, Dinsmore says, is "Here's this thing I'm doing. What do you think?"

"It serves a number of purposes," he explains. "One is it allows other team members to see what other people are doing. And two, it gives people a chance to present it before the time where they're actually on the spot. But it also allows us to say, 'Oh, well, what about this?' or, 'Is this the right way?'"

They sometimes invite people from outside the group that might have a useful outside perspective that can inform their thinking. "You're also looking for happy accidents," he says. "And it happens fairly regularly. It's like, 'oh, there's this piece of information that someone else has been working on over here, and it explains that other topic that I've been thinking about over there.'" He finds, "You can repurpose a lot of things between groups because they're looking at things from different perspectives, but sometimes looking at the same problem."

Dinsmore has a PhD in political science, and he explains, "The mental model for me is a grad school seminar. It's never quite exactly the way I want, but it does do a lot of things in terms of sharing information and perspectives."

Getting input from others takes time and effort, but it often pays off handsomely, producing great insights that are more actionable across the organization. Simply consulting with others, however, is no guarantee of freedom from blinkered thinking. There is a bias that can be introduced that is often referred to as groupthink or "tribal think."

You must be right, you think like me

Groupthink or conforming to a consensus point of view can have disastrous results—and it is glaringly obvious in some intelligence failures.

In a book chapter entitled "Why Bad Things Happen to Good Analysts," former CIA analyst and educator Jack Davis explains, "One example of tribal think came several months before the battering of the Berlin Wall. A CIA analyst circulated a draft assessment that argued that the well-known obstacles to German reunification were no longer strong enough to keep the issue of reunification 'off the table.' This was a bold and prescient departure from the CIA's prevailing expert opinion. His well-informed and well-intentioned colleagues each asked for 'small changes' to avoid an overstatement of the case here and a misinterpretation of the case there. After the coordination process had finished its watering down of the original conclusions by the mending of 'small errors,' a senior reviewer delivered the coup de grâce by all but eliminating the innovative argument from the paper's key judgments. A reader of the final version of the paper would have to delve deeply into the text to uncover the paradigm-breaking analysis.

"In another case, in 1983, eight years before the Soviet Union collapsed, an analyst invested in extensive research and an innovative methodology to conclude that strikes, riots, and other forms of civil unrest were a harbinger of substantial instability. A host of Soviet experts within the CIA strongly resisted this departure from the established position that there was no serious threat to regime stability. The original text was watered down considerably during nearly six months of debate. Even after incorporating numerous changes to accommodate the mindset of the expert critics in CIA, they refused to be associated with even the watered-down assessment, which was then published by the National Intelligence Council without the formal concurrence of the CIA analysts."

The watering down of conclusions can come from consultation within a too narrow range of opinions, or from within a highly politicized environment. If you take a wooden fork and sand down all the dangerously spikey bits, you end up with a spoon. The utility of the original idea can easily be lost.

Do you want ice with that?

Sometimes, however, what seems like watering down is instead bringing a perspective that serves as a tonic. A former CIA analyst and current educator described how the review process worked. "Between me and the President [of the United States] were seven different layers," he explained. "And the hope there is that each has a different function. And so, one layer is to check my grammar and that sort of thing, which hopefully would go fairly quickly. Another layer might be statistical kinds of stuff; you know, if I've cited statistics and numbers and what not, are those accurate, and do the columns all add up? And that's the mechanical lower levels. Then, as it gets up higher and higher and higher, it's more the organizational and the political aspect of it. Did we consider all factors? You know, it's not the analyst's job to think about budgets and personnel and that sort of thing, but at the senior levels, they do have to think about that, and that all has to be worked into it.

"One quick anecdote in this regard: my very first supervisor when I started at the Agency told this wonderful story about when he was a new, young analyst. He was working on something and was convinced that he had some worthwhile insight into it. So, he wrote this piece and started it up this vertical chain, the six or seven people who would have to review it. What he thought was, in the process, his insight was being diluted and lost as other people were trying to get in all their stuff.

"He was very new, very young, very self-confident, and didn't understand how these things all worked and was very impatient with them. And so, he saw it sort of being destroyed as it went up. The final layer of review was somebody on what, at the Agency, is known as the seventh floor, and this is the executive level, where the director and everybody have their offices. And the final sign-off on this was a very, very senior official at the Agency. Not the Director, but somebody just right below them. And the analyst was informed the senior official was going over his stuff, and so he went up to his office.

"He got in the elevator and went up to his office! And of course, they didn't know each other. So, he said, 'I'm the analyst who wrote that piece, and I think it's been distorted and lost.' And the senior official, to his credit, was very patient. I think he'd probably seen it before. And at some point, my colleague said, politely and respectfully, 'You people up here on the seventh floor just don't understand what it's like down in the trenches.' And this very senior guy just paused for a moment, and he said, 'We all have our trenches.'

"This analyst, not aware of all the stuff that's going on in Congress and public relations and all of this, was too focused on his particular narrow piece of the pie."

Sometimes you don't know what you don't know. Consulting widely can reveal your blind spots.

Chapter 12: I doubt that

"Doubt is an uncomfortable condition, but certainty is a ridiculous one." Voltaire.

Doubt is another powerful tool for detecting and correcting error. It might appear as critical thinking or alternative hypotheses or metacognition or reflective practice or devil's advocacy, but the beating heart of all these approaches is doubt.

"William James used to preach the 'will to believe,'" said British philosopher and Nobel Laureate Bertrand Russell. "For my part, I should wish to preach the 'will to doubt.' None of our beliefs are quite true; all have at least a penumbra of vagueness and error. The methods of increasing the degree of truth in our beliefs are well known; they consist in hearing all sides, trying to ascertain all the relevant facts, controlling our own bias by discussion with people who have the opposite bias, and cultivating a readiness to discard any hypothesis which has proved inadequate."

Doubt has a bad rap. It seems negative. But wielded wisely it can be a powerful tool. "Your doubt may become a good quality if you train it," wrote Austrian poet and novelist Rainer Maria Rilke. "It must become knowing, it must become critical. Ask it, whenever it wants to spoil something for you, why something is ugly, demand proofs from it, test it, and you will find it perplexed and embarrassed perhaps, or perhaps rebellious. But don't give in, insist on arguments and act this way, watchful and consistent, every single time, and the day will arrive when from a destroyer [doubt] will become one of your best workers...."

Carl Sagan was an American astronomer and science popularizer who advocated for active skepticism. As part of his "baloney detection kit" he suggested, "Spin more than one hypothesis. If there's something to be explained, think of all the different ways in which it could be explained. Then think of tests by which you might systematically disprove each of the alternatives. What survives, the hypothesis that resists disproof in this Darwinian selection among 'multiple working hypotheses,' has a much better chance of being the right answer than if you had simply run with the first idea that caught your fancy."

He advocated being ready to a reject a hypothesis, even if it is a favorite, because "It's only a way station in the pursuit of knowledge. Ask yourself why you like the idea. Compare it fairly with the alternatives. See if you can find reasons for rejecting it. If you don't, others will."

Law professor Alafair Burke feels doubt is necessary to get past the bias that could lead to a wrongful conviction. "To neutralize confirmation bias," she says, "a prosecutor reviewing a file should not only look for evidence supporting the defendant's guilt, but also scrutinize the case with the eye of a defense attorney searching for reasonable doubt. To mitigate selective information processing, the prosecutor should not simply accept evidence that appears inculpatory; instead, she should force herself to articulate any basis for skepticism. Similarly, she should not just assume that seemingly exculpatory evidence is fabricated or unreliable; she should force herself to anticipate its value to the defense."

Doubt is taught in intelligence analysis programs. "One thing—and I teach specific classes on this—is always to have multiple explanations or outcomes," a professor of intelligence analysis explained. "One of the other drawbacks of the way that your mind works as a pattern-making machine is once you settle on something, then it's hard to shake you from that.

"Ask 'What are four or five possible explanations of this?' And some of that might be what the analyst brings to it, some of it might be what the customers bring to it, some of it might be what the adversaries bring to it, some of it might be historical things that have happened. In history and political science, there are some things that are just more possible than others, and we know this from experience. And by the time you start rattling down that list, you're going to get four or five different possible explanations for it. And then that's how you use your data, is to try and figure out, among those different possibilities, which is the one that matches the data the best? And, of course, this is Heuer's analysis of competing hypotheses in a nutshell."

I think I think about thinking

Doubt, in the form of metacognition—or thinking about thinking—has been proven beneficial in debiasing in medicine. O'Sullivan and Schofield write, "Metacognition is the awareness of, and insight into, one's own thought processes. Forcing clinicians to ask themselves 'what else could this be?' is a form of metacognition and may force one to consider 'why' one is pursuing certain diagnoses, and consider important alternative scenarios. There are a number of positive studies supporting the role of metacognition in improving decision-making."

Similarly, Graber et al. found that "Considering…alternatives improved accuracy and reduced the tendency for subjects to be overconfident in their answers. Similarly, physicians evaluating a difficult test case were more likely to trust a diagnosis when asked to consider alternatives."

They also reported that what they called "reflective practice" or a "diagnostic time out" had been proven to have debiasing effects. "Reflective practice," they explain, "promotes metacognition and incorporates four distinct elements: Seeking out alternative explanations, exploring the consequences of alternative diagnoses, being open to tests that would differentiate the various possibilities and accepting uncertainty. This process, essentially getting a second opinion from your own conscious mind, has the potential to avoid many of the inherent pitfalls of heuristic thought."

This thinking twice, sometimes charmingly called the "wisdom of the inner crowd," has also been proven to increase the accuracy of forecasts. Philip Tetlock and Dan Gardner, writing in *Superforecasting*, report that "merely asking people to assume their judgement is wrong, to seriously consider why that might be, and then make another judgement, produces a second estimate which, when combined with the first, improves accuracy almost as much as getting a second opinion from another person."

Philosopher Friedrich Nietzsche held doubt in much higher esteem than conviction: "A very popular error: having the courage of one's convictions; rather, it is a matter of having the courage for an attack on one's convictions!"

Look at the whole

Dr. Arvi Grover is a cardiologist who is troubled by many physicians' willingness to accept or even embrace WYSIATI—the assumption that what you see is all there is. He sees it as being a problem of a system that encourages blinkered thinking, combined with a tendency to rush to judgement.

Physicians are typically paid per consultation. Some physicians— conscious of this—have posted signs in their clinics saying things like, "For your safety and ours, please limit the discussion with your provider to one issue per visit," and encourage people to make additional appointments.

Samantha Angus of Selkirk, Manitoba visited a doctor who had this policy. She went to her doctor complaining of back pain. When Samantha tried to tell the doctor that she was also having problems with her heart, "the doctor just tapped her wristwatch and said, 'One appointment, one problem,'" her husband Bruce Angus told CBC News. "My wife didn't even get to mention what the problem was. The doctor got up and walked out of the office."

Two weeks later, Bruce was watching television with Samantha, his wife of 32 years, when "all of a sudden, she just fell over in her chair and she was gone," he said. She had died of a heart attack.

Dr. Grover finds that too often "physicians just focus on one complaint and they'll miss the other factors. If someone has palpitations, for instance, and they don't ask about any other problems, they can miss the diagnosis." He feels "medicine has evolved significantly and has become overly reliant on testing rather than our own medical acumen. It becomes much easier to spend a few minutes with a patient and send them for a bunch of tests. But you lack the ability to put all of the pieces together." This sets up perfect conditions for WYSIATI to flourish and develop into a full-blown case of tunnel vision.

To combat this, he prescribes open-ended history taking, treating the patient as a complete being and appreciating the limitations of a narrow test. "The art of history taking and the art of communication are not what they used to be. People are multidimensional. Everyone I encounter is unique. You need to be able to give them the due diligence, listening to them."

"You can't diagnose rot in a tree by looking at just one branch," he explains. "You need to step back and look at the other branches too. An effective problem solver should look at the whole tree, not just a problem branch. We need to step back and look at the larger picture. We can't be tunnel-visioned on any task. People die as a result."

We in the insights industry also need to think past the survey and markers of statistical significance. We need to include competitive intelligence, social media, news, blogs and any other relevant information we can get our hands on. That will help ensure we don't get infected by WYSIATI and develop tunnel vision.

Bagging the Truth

A valuable lesson about looking at the big picture, and not relying solely on self-reports, comes from Southwest Airlines. When everyone in the airline industry started charging for baggage, Southwest Airlines naturally had to consider their position. Paul Sacco, Director, Customer Intelligence for Southwest Airlines, said, "The simple math was that it was worth a lot of money." Charging baggage fees is a quick and easy way to raise additional revenue, and all the airlines were jumping on the bandwagon. But Southwest—which has long prided itself on being a customer-focused airline—wanted to understand how customers might feel if they too imposed baggage fees.

Their initial work asked people how they would react to the addition of baggage fees. No one liked it, but traveler surveys suggested they would get used to it—especially since all the other airlines were doing it too. But that didn't quite sit right with the team. They felt that just taking people at their word might not be getting at the real story. "When we dug in a bit more," Sacco explained, "there was a lot of emotion in it. It really set people off." They interviewed behavioral analytics experts and applied system dynamics modeling to understand the longer-term implications of making a change, which revealed that adding baggage fees would have negative long-term effects. But relying on that was not enough.

Sacco said they had previously noted, "Every time we had raised prices, we'd seen volume drop." So, they modeled what the income gain might be and "put that alongside the revenue that would be at risk. When we did that, the loss dwarfed the amount of money we'd get from bag fees." Southwest still does not charge baggage fees and their CEO has affirmed they have no intention of doing so. And they remain one of the highest rated airlines in terms of customer satisfaction.

It's a great example of how not taking people's responses at face value, coupled with innovative techniques and the use of multiple sources of information and insights, saved an organization from falling for a brand-damaging, short-term cash grab. In addition to powering our analysis with a wide range of inputs, we need to look for what is not there.

The sound of silence

Heuer earlier alluded to the story of the dog that did not bark in the nighttime. That is a reference to Sir Arthur Conan Doyle's Sherlock Holmes story "Silver Blaze." It is about the mysterious disappearance of a racehorse. It is believed by Scotland Yard that a stranger stole the horse, but Holmes is convinced it was horse's late trainer, John Straker—because of what did not happen:

> Gregory (Scotland Yard detective): "Is there any other point to which you would wish to draw my attention?"
> Holmes: "To the curious incident of the dog in the nighttime."
> Gregory: "The dog did nothing in the nighttime."
> Holmes: "That was the curious incident."

Holmes says, "I had grasped the significance of the silence of the dog, for one true inference invariably suggests others.... Obviously the midnight visitor was someone whom the dog knew well. It was Straker who removed Silver Blaze from his stall and led him out on to the moor."

Knowing just how pernicious WYSIATI can be, a professor of intelligence analysis offers advice that could have come straight from Sherlock Holmes. He admonishes analysts to "not be distracted by what you see and hear and miss the chance to think about, 'Oh, what's not there? What am I not seeing?'"

"Confront all seemingly impossible scenarios," urges Rolf Dobelli in his book *The Art of Thinking Clearly*. "What unexpected events might happen? What lurks behind the burning issues? What is no one addressing? Pay attention to silences as much as you respond to noises. Check the periphery, not just the center. Think the unthinkable. Something unusual can be huge; we still may not see it. Being big and distinctive is not enough to be seen. The unusual and huge thing must be expected."

In the world of insights, we need to consider why there were no differences and what questions we did not ask. When we look at the results of a driver analysis and it explains one-third of why people buy, it should serve as a prompt for us to consider what other factors are driving the market. Are they addressable factors we need to understand? Are there structural factors we need to comprehend?

In multi-stage iterative research programs, stopping to ponder what is not there can help solve the problem of "noise neglect," as highlighted by Tetlock, Mandel, and others. In that situation, the errors or noise "in the conclusions from the one stage get fed into the next." In listening for the silence of what is not there in multi-stage projects, prick up your ears for the noise of earlier erroneous assumptions.

Taking time to think about what is absent is challenging. There is nothing to look at, no numbers to crunch, no tests to suggest significance. Nothing.

But making the space to contemplate what the possibilities are can be vitally important.

Look at the hole

A story involving U.S. Bombers, Air Force Generals and a Columbia University statistician illustrates the power of thinking about what you are not seeing. The year was 1943, and many, many bomber aircraft were being shot down. The Allies were searching for ways to improve the odds that their bombers would make it home safely. The obvious idea was to place more armor on them, but they couldn't armor the whole plane. It would be too heavy. They needed to be selective. So, they collected data on where the bullet holes were in each returning bomber. The Air Force top brass reasoned that where the bullets holes were was where they should place the armor, because that was clearly where the planes were being shot up. Fortunately, they consulted Columbia's Statistical Research Group.

A brilliant statistician there named Abraham Wald pointed out what they weren't seeing: the planes that had not made it back. The aircraft they had examined, which had all survived their missions, were revealing where the planes could absorb enemy fire and still fly. His insight was that they should add more armor to the parts of the plane where there were no bullet holes. It was the hits in those places that were bringing planes down.

Seeing what was missing made all the difference. As the son of a WWII Royal Air Force bombardier who survived countless missions despite being shot up, I am particularly grateful Dr. Wald took the time to think about what was not there.

Chapter 13: Check it out

"I watch a lot of astronaut movies…Mostly Star Wars. And even Han and Chewie use a checklist."
Jon Stewart

Things like checklists, or the grid structure used in the CIA's ACH, are attempts to ensure things are not overlooked. Checklists, by their nature, require you to consider things you might gloss over or forget to consider. They help when faced with complex situations or when quick problem solving is necessary.

Atul Gawande is a surgeon, writer, and public health researcher. He and his colleagues have focused their research on problems at the intersection of surgery and public health. Much of their work has examined error in surgery, establishing its frequency and seriousness and revealing underlying mechanisms. His work on detecting patterns of error and identifying ways to correct those errors led him to learn from fields as diverse as building engineering, aviation, and high-end restaurants. They all pointed him to the value of checklists. His work on developing checklists for surgery has saved thousands of lives around the world. He tells the story of discovering the value of checklists very compellingly in his book *The Checklist Manifesto: How to Get Things Right*.

He believes checklists can be helpful anywhere people make mistakes. That never happens with insights professionals, right? He writes, "We don't study routine failures in teaching, in law, in government programs, the financial industry, or elsewhere. We don't look for the patterns of our recurrent mistakes or devise and refine potential solutions for them.

"But we could, and that's the ultimate point. We are all plagued by failures—by missed subtleties, overlooked knowledge, and outright errors. For the most part, we have imagined that little can be done beyond working harder and harder to catch the problems and clean up after them. We are not in the habit of thinking the way the army pilots did as they looked upon their shiny new Model 299 bomber—a machine so complex no one was sure human beings could fly it." This 1935 bomber, better known as the "Flying Fortress," crashed on its maiden flight in front of a crowd of generals who were ready to order a fleet of them. This prompted engineers to pioneer the use of checklists in aviation, to manage the plane's complexity.

"They too could have decided just to 'try harder' or to dismiss a crash as the failings of a 'weak' pilot. Instead they chose to accept their fallibilities. They recognized the simplicity and power of using a checklist."

Gawande sees the use of checklists as a process check and a catch-safe that can reorient you and help you manage complexity. As he writes, checklists "cannot fly a plane. Instead they provide reminders of only the most critical and important steps."

Checklists can help, but when they or other structured processes become limiting or a bureaucratic crutch, they become problematic.

Just check the box

One criticism of ACH and other structured analytic techniques is that they box people in, discourage exploratory thinking, and give people a minimum they can strive for while proving they have "done what they were supposed to do." In other words, structured analytic processes— when poorly designed and misused—can dumb things down.

We can purloin good ideas from other sense-makers that we can weave into the world of insights. But we can also learn how well-intentioned but misguided approaches limit the value of research.

Archeologists have standards akin to an SAT or a checklist. A significant proportion of archaeological consulting work is focused on cultural resource management. The aim is to identify the implications of building roads, structures, or anything that might disturb cultural heritage that is underground or underwater. These archeologists are government-regulated and must adhere to very specific standards and guidelines. Their work is far from the swashbuckling pursuits of Indiana Jones. But they are detectives, making sense of what is underground based on small samples of digging, ground-penetrating radar, historical research, and deduction. It's a fascinating mixture of relatively sparse quantitative and qualitative information that must be synthesized into a conclusion about the significance of a site.

Scarlett Janusas is a land and underwater archaeologist, with experience in both prehistoric and historic archaeology, and over 40 years' field, lab, report, and management experience. She works all over Canada, but much of her work is in Ontario, where she is regulated by the standards of the Ministry of Tourism, Culture and Sport. The standards are, she told me, "very strict and tell us what to write, how to write, what data to collect. There's not a lot of leeway there."

The standards prescribe "how you must do a stage one, which is background research; stage two, feet on the ground; stage three, site specific mitigation; and stage four, avoidance or full excavation. They're very specific in what you do, how many squares you dig, how big your holes are, how you write your report," she explained.

"I think a lot of us grapple with this imposed specification of how we're supposed to write a report. Our title page is even dictated to us. How we write our resources section is dictated to us. They've given us a space for a title, and you've got to fill it in, and your maps all have to be in the back. They can't be interjected right after you mention them in the report or table or something like that. It's very restrictive."

Surprised by how templated the analysis was, I asked her why these analytic standards had been created. She explained, "The Ministry had determined, and rightly so, that there were many consultants who were doing less than adequate work. They wouldn't include photos, they wouldn't include location information, the recommendations were often out of sync with what should have been recommended. I've seen some of these earlier reports and it's not bare minimum, it's negligible information and very poor archeology." That sounds a lot like the often uneven quality of work that is done in the insights industry.

I asked her about the impact of these standards on the quality of archeology that is done. She suggested that, in terms of creating a consistent historical record, it was positive. But in terms of generating a penetrating understanding of the significance of a site, it was negative. "I think it's better for the archaeological resources in general," she said, "because they are being reported at the level of consistency where you can go back and say, 'yes, I can look for X, Y and Z.' And you know that the work has actually been completed. Because, in the past, people would often not go out to do the site and say they did the site. So, they have to keep proof now that they've done it. In that way, yes, it's a positive.

"In terms of the creative process, it's very negative, I think. The Ministry want what they've laid out, and when you give them too much information they often go, 'I don't know what to do with this,' and they send it back. This has happened to both my colleague Sue and me. We write wonderful historical accounts and talk about the data in certain ways and interpret it and they're going, 'No, we don't understand, therefore you're wrong, and take it out.'"

"You provide very few, if any, insights using that kind of a formula. I find that frustrating because I like to do a bit more than what's being asked for. I don't think a minimum is a good way to set a standard."

In archeology in Canada we have an attempt to encourage a higher standard of analysis that half succeeded but has had unforeseen, unfortunate side effects. It's a valuable cautionary tale as we think about how structured analytic techniques and checklists could benefit the insights industry. Being overly prescriptive can unwittingly produce problems.

Paying for the privilege

But you can't keep a curious archeologist down, at least not Scarlett. She is so interested in unearthing insights that she pays for it out of her own pocket. "What I try to do is allow my staff, and myself, to explore some of our more interesting projects. For example, we just did a job in Brantford last year and we were doing some urban brownfield archeology in a whole block. Half of the block had standing buildings and another half was subject to the archaeological assessment, and we were able to play with the data a bit because we're talking about neighborhood archeology. We looked at how neighbors had interacted with each other, and the block as a whole, and then how it compared to the city or neighboring blocks."

They found "there was some competition between each of the neighbors—a keeping up with the Jones's kind of a thing." "You could see when they were trading things amongst themselves, whether they were eating the same kind of foodstuffs, who had the higher end cut of meat versus the lower end," she explained. "And we could identify who was working out of their home. And at the time, of course, there was no garbage pickup, so the backyards were a literal goldmine for us.

"The people on this block also shared backyards. They were obviously doing some recreational meet-and-greet in the backyard, and so there was a lot of coming and going. And neighbors were probably better neighbors than in urban centers these days, where everyone has a fence up in their backyard. There were no fences. That, for sure, we know. We stripped the ground and no fences were erected. So, people shared a common backyard. They each had their own privy in the backyard. But you could see that they interacted with each other, which was neat, because you don't often get to do that kind of analysis."

Scarlett's thirst for insights led her to work above and beyond the standards, spend her own time and money, and make the effort to write and present three papers based on this project at an archeological conference. As a result, she opened a window on a previously hidden piece of history.

That's the kind of insights professional I admire.

I don't need to check out checklists

Something as simple as a checklist can seem trivial and potentially useful only for people without much experience. And we're experienced researchers, right? That's what Dr. Gawande thought too.

"In the spring of 2007, as soon as our surgery checklist began taking form, I began using it in my own operations. I did so not because I thought it was needed but because I wanted to make sure it was really usable. Also, I did not want to be a hypocrite. We were about to trot this thing out in eight cities around the world. I had better be using it myself. But in my heart of hearts—if you strapped me down and threatened to take out my appendix without anesthesia unless I told the truth—did I think the checklist would make much of a difference in my cases? No. In *my* cases? Please.

"To my chagrin, however, I have yet to get through a week in surgery without the checklists leading us to catch something we would have missed. Take last week, as I write this, for instance. We had three catches in five cases."

One patient had not been given the antibiotic she needed. A second one was almost given an antibiotic she should not have received. In a third case, the checklist caught the fact that a woman receiving thyroid surgery had difficulty breathing following prior surgeries—once even ending up in intensive care. Dr. Gawande had not been aware of this until the checklist surfaced it. Once cognizant, the team were able to plan to give her inhalers before and after surgery and to monitor her overnight. Gawande wrote that the inhalers "worked beautifully. She never needed extra oxygen at all."

So what?

We have seen that, because we learn by making connections to what have learned before, it is seductively simple for us to fall into the trap of making easy connections that make sense but in fact are wrong. Our brains are pattern-seeking machines that will find patterns even in randomness. And the unthinking use of statistical tests can exacerbate that problem. We have biases that lead us to confirm our expectations, sometimes blinding us to the truth.

Obtaining a full and accurate understanding or a market, culture or nation is hard. We need to be aware of where we can go wrong, so that we can identify and hopefully correct our misperceptions. Getting feedback on past studies, being collaborative and working more in teams, embracing doubt, and using checklists are all useful correctives, our fellow sense-makers suggest.

So how do we move forward? Law professor Ian Weinstein has some sober-minded advice: "We should not believe everything we think, but we should believe much of what we think, especially if we can develop the habit of checking up on ourselves."

Check out

In the spirit of checking up on ourselves, here is a checklist to help us learn, detect problems and get closer to an accurate insight. It is very simple, and its value has yet to be quantitatively proven, but experience suggests it is effective.

The time to use the checklist is before starting analysis. Use it to guide your next steps. Then use it again, when you have done your preliminary analysis and before sending the report or giving the presentation.

BIAS DETECTION CHECKLIST	Yes	No
Did we learn from feedback from prior projects?	☐	☐
Did we get input on our preliminary thinking and ideas for insights from a diverse team?	☐	☐
Did we actively doubt our conclusions?	☐	☐
Did we actively consider and test out multiple ideas, not just our initial conclusion?	☐	☐
Do we have a broad range of evidence—including from outside our research—to support our conclusions, or are we riskily reliant on a few pieces of information?	☐	☐

It's simple, but sometimes simplicity is what you need.

Having looked at the challenges associated with getting to an insight, let's now turn to the fun part: generating insights.

Chapter 14: Generating insights

"Insights are like cats. They can be coaxed but usually don't come when called."
John Kounios and Mark Beeman

Picture a black jaguar stealthily stalking through trees and brush: thrilling, powerful, elusive, and startling when it emerges into view—that's an insight. The moment of unveiling an understanding that had eluded us is why we get up in the morning. There is something supremely satisfying in having that last piece of the puzzle snap into place, revealing the full picture. But beyond the intellectual pleasure involved, insights open the door to opportunity.

Whether it be discovering a way to reduce fire fatalities, or how to get noticed on a crowded shelf, insights light the way. Connections between fresh insights give birth to scientific, industrial, and intellectual revolutions. The invention of the printing press, novel ideas on international trade, and a healthy disregard for any barriers between art, architecture, and science all fueled the Renaissance. The echoes of that insight-driven intellectual big bang still reverberate today. But not all insights result in such explosions.

Insights come in all shapes and sizes. Some upend the way we understand the world, while others make it easier to open a bottle of wine. They all, however, follow a similar pattern. By discerning that design, we can better coax insights to emerge from the dusky forest and stand blinking in the warming light of dawn.

Insights, while mysterious, can be brought to light through the application of a deliberate process and with specific mindsets. Our understanding of how insights work has, appropriately, been the result of people building on each other's insights about insights. Two important early thinkers about insights were Hermann Helmholtz and

Henri Poincaré, both of whom were polymaths—people who made connections across disciplines.

Cake anyone?

Hermann Ludwig Ferdinand von Helmholtz, described as Germany's greatest scientist of the nineteenth century, was a physician, physiologist, and physicist who effortlessly crossed the boundaries of many disciplines. He helped prove the law of conservation of energy, invented the ophthalmoscope (which allows optometrists to look into your eyes—you've probably experienced one), constructed a generalized form of electrodynamics, and foresaw the atomic structure of electricity. He anticipated the existence of radio waves, which was later proven by one of his students, Heinrich Hertz.

The largest German association of research institutions, the Helmholtz Association, is named in honor of him. There is also an asteroid named after him, as well as craters on both the moon and Mars. It's fair to say he had quite an impact.

On his 70th birthday, August 31, 1891, there were national celebrations, a biography was published, and there was a congratulatory dinner at which he spoke. That night, his description of how he arrived at insights was classic; it is reported, in English, in pioneering psychologist Robert Woodworth's seminal *Experimental Psychology*:

"Often…[ideas] arrived suddenly, without any effort on my part, like an inspiration.…They never came to a fatigued brain and never at my writing desk. It was always necessary, first of all, that I should have turned my problem over on all sides to such an extent that I had all angles and complexities 'in my head'.…Then there must come an hour of complete physical freshness and quiet wellbeing, before the good ideas arrived. Often they were there in the morning when I first awoke…but they liked especially to make their appearance while I was taking an easy walk over wooded hills in sunny weather."

Formation of Fuchsian functions

Henri Poincaré was a French mathematician, theoretical physicist, engineer, and philosopher of science who taught at the Sorbonne in Paris, starting in 1881. Poincaré made important contributions to thinking on celestial mechanics, fluid mechanics, optics, electricity, telegraphy, capillarity, elasticity, thermodynamics, potential theory, quantum theory, theory of relativity, and physical cosmology. In his book *Science and Method* he describes a wonderful series of insights that came to him while he was struggling with Fuchsian functions:

"For a fortnight I had been attempting to prove that there could not be any function analogous to what I have since called Fuchsian functions….Every day I sat down at my table and spent an hour or two trying a great number of combinations and I arrived at no result. One night I took some black coffee, contrary to my custom, and was unable to sleep. A host of ideas kept surging in my head. I could almost feel them jostling one another, until two of them coalesced, so to speak, to form a stable combination. When morning came, I had established the existence of one class of Fuchsian functions, those that are derived from hyper-geometric series."

Note how he turns the problem over in his mind and considers what Helmholtz calls the "angles and complexities" before taking a break and having an idea surface. Poincaré then "left Caen, where I was living, to take part in a geological conference arranged by the School of Mines. The incidents of the journey made me forget my mathematical work. When we arrived at Constance, we got into a [vehicle] to go for a drive, and, just as I put my foot on the step, the idea came to me, though nothing in my former thoughts seemed to have prepared me for it, that the transformations I had used to define Fuchsian functions were identical with those of non-Euclidian geometry." Again: engagement, rest, and boom!

Later, he says, "I then began to study arithmetical questions without any great apparent result, and without suspecting they could have the least connection with my previous researches. Disgusted by my want of success, I went away to spend a few days at the seaside, and thought of entirely different things. One day, as I was walking on the cliff, an idea came to me, again with the same characteristics of conciseness, suddenness, and immediate certainty, that arithmetical transformations of indefinite ternary quadratic forms are identical to those of non-Euclidian geometry." Once more, the effort, the break, and the formation of new connections that led to seemingly sudden insight.

Having returned home, and proved out his insight, Poincaré found there was one function that he could not find the solution for. He says, "all my efforts were of no avail at first, except to make me better understand the difficulty, which was already something. All this work was perfectly conscious.... Thereupon I left for Mont-Valérien, where I had to serve my time in the army and so my mind was preoccupied with very different matters. One day, as I was crossing the street, the solution of the difficulty that had brought me to a standstill came to me all at once."

"One is at once struck," he wrote, "by these appearances of sudden illumination, obvious indications of a long course of unconscious work.... Often when a man is working at a difficult question, he accomplishes nothing the first time he sets to work. Then he takes more or less of a rest, and then sits down again at his table. During the first half-hour he still finds nothing, and then all at once the decisive idea presents itself to his mind. We might say that the conscious work proved more fruitful because it was interrupted and the rest restored force and freshness to the mind. But it is more probable that the rest was occupied with unconscious work, and that the result of this work was afterward revealed...."

His insight about the unconscious at work was very prescient and has, in subsequent years, been proven to have a firm basis in neurological function, as we shall see later. The recurring process of effort, rest, and revelation is also a powerful theme.

The art of thought

Graham Wallas, a social psychologist and one of the founders of the London School of Economics, drew upon the observations of Helmholtz and Poincaré for his timeless 1926 book *The Art of Thought*. In it he describes a model of the process of generating insights. He lays out four stages: preparation, incubation, illumination, and verification.

Preparation is where Poincaré "sat down at my table and spent an hour or two trying a great number of combinations" and when Helmholtz "turned my problem over on all sides to such an extent that I had all angles and complexities 'in my head.'" For the insights industry, it is when we marinate our minds in all the data, observations, social media analysis, blogs posts, journal articles, industry news, critics' perspectives, and whatever else flavors our investigations.

When Poincaré writes, "Disgusted by my want of success, I went away to spend a few days at the seaside," he is describing the incubation stage. Illumination happens for Helmholtz "while I was taking an easy walk over wooded hills in sunny weather." And Poincaré describes verification when he says, "Naturally, I proposed to form all these functions. I laid siege to them systematically and captured all the outworks one after the other."

While Wallas's four step process of preparation, incubation, illumination, and verification is very enduring, it was usefully extended by advertising executive James Webb Young in his 1940 classic *A Technique for Producing Ideas*, which is still in print today. Inspired by Wallas and Poincaré, Young subdivided the preparation stage into two parts: the gathering of information and the process of working. For our purposes it is a useful distinction, and in the following chapters we'll follow Young's model as we explore how to coax out insights.

Industrializing insights

Young's writing reflects the optimism of an era in which industrialization was revolutionizing what people did and how they imagined. He asserts "that the production of ideas is just as definite a process as the production of Fords; that the production of ideas, too, runs on an assembly line; that in this production the mind follows an operative technique which can be learned and controlled; and that its effective use is just as much a matter of practice in the technique as is the effective use of any tool."

With a copywriter's crispness, Young distills the generation of insights into five steps:

"First, the gathering of raw materials—both the materials of your immediate problem and the materials which come from a constant enrichment of your store of general knowledge.

Second, the working of these materials over in your mind.

Third, the incubating stage, where you let something beside the conscious mind do the work of synthesis.

Fourth, the actual birth of the Idea—the 'Eureka! I have it!' stage.

And fifth, the final shaping and development of the idea to practical usefulness."

Young's steps make generating insights seem almost formulaic. But we should listen to pioneering scientist Francis Bacon when he says, "The lame in the path outstrip the swift who wander from it."

What's not immediately apparent in Young's elegant model is how crucial the mindset we bring to it is. Open-mindedness, a willingness to take risks, allowing yourself space for ideas to percolate, suspending disbelief, and embracing the unexpected are all essential.

Phil Beadle, a U.K. educator, has written a book on creativity wonderfully titled *Dancing about Architecture*. He writes about the open mindset needed to creatively hunt insights, saying, "if we are prepared to experiment, to focus on process and let 'outcome' float around on the breeze waiting to be discovered, something different happens. We either fall flat on our behinds, or we discover new lands; and you cannot discover new lands by keeping one foot in the old country. So jump, happily, knowing that the process of learning to be brilliant involves risk….It is always worth taking a risk. Your audience will forgive you if it doesn't work. They will feel the thrill of the high wire along with you when they walk it."

Let's make the leap and explore each of Young's five steps on the journey to producing insights.

Chapter 15: Gather raw materials

"Reading about nature is fine, but if a person walks in the woods and listens carefully, he can learn more than what is in books...."
George Washington Carver

The way insights come together gives us some hints about how to best approach the information-gathering phase. Steve Johnston, in *Where Good Ideas Come From,* describes it this way: "A good idea is a network. A specific constellation of neurons—thousands of them—fire in sync with each other for the first time in your brain, and an idea pops into your consciousness. A new idea is a network of cells exploring the adjacent possible of connections that they can make in your mind. This is true whether the idea in question is a new way to solve a complex physics problem, or a closing line for a novel, or a feature for a software application. If we're going to try to explain the mystery of where ideas come from, we have to shake ourselves free of this common misconception: an idea is not a single thing. It is more like a swarm."

In this network, the neurons are repositories of past knowledge, feelings and experiences. This image of a connected constellation evokes a vision of a vast network of previous learnings now connected in new and different ways. Picturing this, it becomes clear that the more sources involved, the more connections, and the more varied the insights can be.

Making connections

Check out the following diagram. Picture the one dot as a single study. With no context, no connection to other information, it is sad, lonely, and unable to generate an insight. With two pieces of information a connection is possible, but just one. Even three just allows us to generate three connections. We start cruising when we hit four, five allows us to get rolling, and then it really starts to take off. By the time we get to 10 we can have 45 combinations. Crank that up to 100 and we have 4,950 possible combinations.

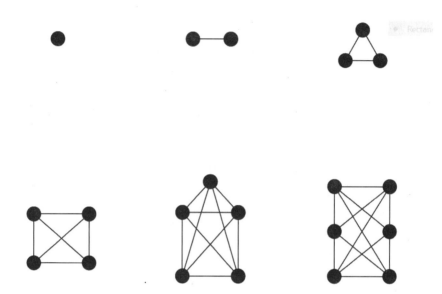

The more information we can absorb, the greater the number of opportunities there are to generate an insight. That's why, when we are gathering raw materials, it is important to tap into multiple information sources, and a variety of them.

In the early days of market research, information was scarce, and the survey was expected to be the primary source. Only by connecting that survey to other knowledge was it possible to generate an insight. Now, there is a deluge of information, and surveys provide just one piece of the puzzle. The unfortunate thing is, the way we report survey results is stuck in the past. Most are simply summaries of what was in the survey, without context and without connections to other information.

"One of the weirdest things market researchers do is present a report that is solely based on the piece of research they just conducted," Ray Poynter of #NewMR told me. "What amazing hubris: to assume your research project on its own is going to answer any meaningful question." Indeed, presenting the results of a survey on its own represents a lost opportunity for generating insights. This is a blinkered practice that limits the value of survey research.

Information omnivores

The fictional detective Sherlock Holmes was famous for his scrapbooks. These scrapbooks were not just artistically arranged collections of memorabilia, they were working documents—a collection of bits and pieces of newspapers, reports, and other tidbits. In both creating and perusing them, Holmes was laying down the raw material for his later insights. His remarkable ability to make connections where others did not was fueled by his omnivorous approach to knowledge. History, manufacturing processes, science, political affairs, and magic tricks were all grist for the mill for Arthur Conan Doyle's character.

Doyle himself was a physician who, in addition to his famous Sherlock Holmes stories, wrote science fiction, fantasy, and humor, as well as plays, romances, poetry, non-fiction, and historical novels. This Scot was also an amateur architect and golf course designer who spoke German. Information omnivore and boundary crosser? Ja.

Science writer Kyla Mandel also believes the more varied the sources, the richer the story. She told me, "I like to use a variety of types of sources for my stories, and I think that all good stories need a mix. From databases to scientific studies and documents—both primary and secondary, contemporary and historical sources—as well as human sources, whether that be individuals who have witnessed or experienced something firsthand or experts in a field. Each type of source brings a different type of information, and together it helps make the question you're trying to answer and story you're telling become clearer and richer. Having a variety of sources allows you to dive into the complexity and nuance of a story."

Young, in his *A Technique for Producing Ideas*, posits, "In advertising an idea results from a combination of *specific knowledge* about products and people with *general knowledge* about life and events." He sees this general knowledge as essential: "Every really good creative person…whom I have ever known has always had two noticeable characteristics. First, there was no subject under the sun in which he could not easily get interested—from, say, Egyptian burial customs to modern art. Every facet of life had fascination for him. Second, he was an extensive browser in all sorts of fields of information. For it is with the advertising man as with the cow: no browsing, no milk." Bovines are herbivores that like to forage widely. Spring clover, sweet. Last year's hay in the barn again? Boring.

The more varied the inputs, the more unique and impactful the insights can be. It is no accident that Helmholtz and Poincaré worked across disciplines, applying knowledge from one area to another. They were information omnivores, and their example points the way.

Note it, and save it

"Part of the secret of hunch cultivation is simple: write everything down," says Steven Johnson. While Sherlock Holmes had his scrapbooks, Charles Darwin had his notebooks. He kept dozens of them, and there are tens of thousands of pages of his notes available today. He jotted down observations, hypotheses, and drafts of ideas, and made drawings. What he cataloged was wide-ranging. In one entry from his trip to the Galapagos, he wrote of a day in Peru, "steaming hot — cascades in all parts, enormous precipices — columnar — covered with Lilies — Bananas & trees — after ascending fern hill threw myself in shade of thick trees surrounded by Sugar — Bananas — — Food so abundant — Yams, Taro — Sweet root like Sugar, size of [log] & forest of shady Bananas."

Beyond the flora, he also made detailed notes about geology: "Hills all soft & worn into that sort of bifurcating ridges which is peculiar to degradation of soft matter; in all the ranges which I saw were composed of very soft gneiss or protogene, which is interlaced by veins of same figure as quartz of a siliceo-Feldspath nature or Trapoidal or semiporphyritic, intersect each other, thin out downwards; & pass in places into surrounding rock."

In addition to geographic features and vegetation, he mentions fauna and their actions and habits: "Iguana — shakes head vertically; sea — one no = dozes, hind legs stretched out walks very slowly — sleeps — closes eyes — Eats much Cactus: Mr Bynoe saw one walking from two other carrying it in mouth — Eats very deliberately, without chewing — Small Finc[h] picking from same piece after alights on back."

What's important about these notebooks is that what he recorded became something he referred to years later, as he worked toward his theory of natural selection and evolution. The idea of evolution did not come to him in the Galapagos. It came years later, aided by his notebooks. He had embarked on the journey to study geology, but because he was omnivorous, he also made enough notes about the animals and vegetation that he had the information to fuel his later insights. So, when you find something interesting, even randomly interesting, squirrel it away. You never know how it might help.

Alternative perspectives

In addition to obtaining a variety of types of information, it is also critical to entertain multiple points of view. Unfortunately, in an internet-driven world, "filter bubbles" narrow what we are exposed to. A filter bubble occurs when websites use algorithms to assume the types of information a user would want to see, based on past activity. Thus, it's all too easy for useful things to go unseen, while the familiar is reinforced. These filter bubbles suppress serendipity by leading us down familiar paths, rather than enabling us to explore foreign lands. Doug Lorch, one of Philip Tetlock's superforecasters, crafted a creative way of bursting the bubble.

Lorch knows the accuracy of his insights is driven by the quality and completeness of the information he uses. Aware that it is easy to resort to consulting his usual sources, Lorch, as Tetlock and Gardner explain in *Superforecasting*, "created a database containing hundreds of information sources—from the *New York Times* to obscure blogs—that are tagged by their ideological orientation, subject matter, and geographical origin….He then wrote a program to select what he should read next using criteria that emphasize diversity. Thanks to Doug's simple invention, he is sure to encounter different perspectives. Doug is not merely open-minded. He is *actively* open-minded."

We might not go to the lengths that Doug Lorch does, but we certainly can ensure that when we read industry news, we also read the views of critics and tap into the thoughts of other disciplines. If we want to identify opportunity in the pet food space, for example, we'd want to hoover up the perspectives of PETA, scan veterinary journals, and read what animal ethicists are saying, in addition to perusing petfoodindustry.com and absorbing the results of some surveys.

Neuroscientists John Kounios and Mark Beeman have seen the effects of being open-minded in brain activity: "Just before a person sees a problem that she will eventually solve by insight, there is greater activity in the temporal lobes of both hemispheres. By itself, this wasn't a big surprise. The temporal lobes, which are near the ears, are involved in processing words and concepts. When a person prepares to solve a verbal puzzle, it makes sense that her brain would get ready by activating its knowledge of words and their meanings. It would also make sense that the temporal lobes of both hemispheres would be primed—this would energize both close and remote associations." As we'll see in more detail in a later chapter, the remote associations are what allow for making unexpected connections that produce unique insights.

Kounios and Beeman also observed that when a person is solving a problem analytically—rather than insightfully—their brain does not fire up the same way in both hemispheres. "The difference," they say, "is that for a person in an insightful frame of mind everything is up for consideration. Nothing is off the table. Any idea—every idea, no matter the source—is considered a potential solution. That's why both the left and right temporal lobes light up like a Christmas tree when a person adopts an insightful mind-set. It's the neural manifestation of openness to the full range of possibilities."

This vision of an open, ready mind underscores the importance of gathering lots of information, from a variety of sources. A mind that lights up like a Christmas tree is ready to take advantage of all available information, the more the merrier.

And now to work

Having gathered information that is both specific and general, and that reflects varied points of view, it is time to move to the next stage—working the materials over in your mind. Of this next stage W.I.B. Beveridge, in *The Art of Scientific Investigation* says, "facts and ideas are dead in themselves and it is the imagination that gives life to them. But dreams and speculations are idle fantasies unless reason turns them to useful purpose. Vague ideas captured on flights of fancy have to be reduced to specific propositions and hypotheses."

Chapter 16: Work the materials over in your mind

"The seeds of great discoveries are constantly floating around us, but they only take root in minds well prepared to receive them."
Joseph Henry

Horace Walpole was born in 1717, the youngest son of British Prime Minister Sir Robert Walpole. He grew up to be the originator of gothic fiction, an art historian, and a member of Parliament. He also coined the word serendipity—the unplanned fortunate discovery. He created this word after reading an ancient Persian tale entitled *The Travels and Adventures of Three Princes of Serendip*. Serendip is the old Persian name for Sri Lanka.

Walpole was also a letter writer, but not of the "Dear Mom, I skinned my knee at camp today" variety. Yale University Press published 48 volumes of his letters on varied subjects, including many written to his distant cousin Horace Mann, a British diplomat in Italy. It is in one of these letters that he coins the word serendipity. He was writing about how he had unexpectedly made an important discovery about a coat of arms by what he called "serendipity."

Walpole writes, "This discovery [was one]…by which I find everything I want, *a`pointe nomm´ee* [at the very moment], wherever I dip for it. This discovery, indeed, is almost of that kind which I call *Serendipity*, a very expressive word, which…I shall endeavour to explain to you….I once read a silly fairy tale, called the three Princes of Serendip: as their Highnesses travelled, they were always making discoveries, by accidents and sagacity…."

The three princes are the sons of Jafer, the philosopher-king of Serendip. In the story, King Jafer's sons receive an education from the wisest men in the kingdom, but Jafer wants the princes to complement that with travel and learning about the customs of other peoples, so he sends them off. They have adventures, generate Sherlock Holmes-like insights and generally bounce about, enjoying many unplanned fortunate discoveries.

Serendipity has a long history in science, music, art, and medicine. In seemingly chance encounters, people make connections they did not expect between things. Consider the story of Alexander Fleming, suffering from a particularly juicy cold, accidentally sneezing into a Petri dish full of bacteria that he was working with. Some days later, he noticed the bacteria in the dish had been destroyed. Intrigued, he went on to isolate what would become the first antibiotic: penicillin.

But discoveries like these are not exactly made by chance. People make them by working through a problem and being open to fresh ideas that suggest answers to that problem. This is the mindset psychologist Kevin Dunbar refers to when he says, "the prepared mind favors chance."

Workin' it

In "working the materials over" the goal is to use analytic reasoning to absorb what you have learned, while mulling over hypotheses. This stage is exploratory and benefits from thinking about the question from as many perspectives as possible.

James Webb Young says that, in this stage, "What you do is take the different bits of material you have gathered and feel them all over, as it were, with the tentacles of the mind. You take one fact, turn it this way and that, look at it in different lights, and feel for the meaning of it. You bring two facts together and see how they fit.

"What you are seeking now is the relationship, a synthesis where everything will come together in a neat combination, like a jigsaw puzzle." As you do this, he says, "little tentative ideas will come to you. Put these down on paper. Never mind how crazy or incomplete they seem: get them down. These are foreshadowings of the real idea that is to come, and expressing these in words forwards the process."

In their book *The Evolution of Physics,* Albert Einstein and Leopold Infeld underscore how important this process is: "The mere formulation of a problem is far more essential than its solution, which may be merely a matter of mathematical or experimental skills. To raise new questions, new possibilities, to regard old problems from a new angle, requires creative imagination and marks real advance in science."

He likes to watch

Kevin Dunbar is an Irishman who did his PhD in psychology at the University of Toronto. He now runs the Laboratory for Thinking, Reasoning, Creativity & Educational Neuroscience at the University of Maryland. He also happens to like hanging around labs, watching scientists work.

His interest is not in the specifics of their experiments, but in how they approach their work. He focuses on how "scientists think, reason and generate new models and theories." Over the course of a decade he investigated how scientists work. He simultaneously conducted "experiments on scientific thinking and model building in my own laboratory. The labs that I have been investigating are molecular biology and immunology laboratories in the U.S., Canada, and Italy."

Beveridge observed, "Elaborate apparatus plays an important part in the science of to-day, but I sometimes wonder if we are not inclined to forget that the most important instrument in research must always be the mind of man." That's what Dunbar and his colleagues attend to.

They join meetings, watch people at work, ask questions, develop their own hypotheses, and run experiments with science students to test out their ideas. Their observations are not just qualitative, however. They take meticulous notes and recordings and code them to provide additional quantitative information. Among the activities they have found to be important are working in teams, analogical reasoning, and attention to unexpected findings. These three are critical in the stage of working the materials over in our minds.

It takes a village

One of the most important ways scientists generate and refine their theories, Dunbar has observed, is through working in teams: "The image of science that we are all familiar with is one of the lone scientist toiling away under a naked light bulb for long hours. Suddenly, inspiration strikes and the scientist has made a discovery. This is the image of science that has motivated much research in cognitive science. Its key features are that the scientist works alone and that scientific discovery occurs in a flash of insight. How representative of contemporary science is this view? Our research and that of other cognitive scientists such as Paul Thagard is revealing that reasoning in science, particularly at the critical moments of hypothesis formation, experimental design, data interpretation, and discovery is by groups of scientists and not individual scientists. We call this type of reasoning distributed reasoning.

"Thus, it is not one scientist shouting 'Eureka,' but a number of scientists building a new model by adding different components to the model." Dunbar has found that "one place where much reasoning and new discoveries are made is at weekly lab meetings. In those meetings…an important feature of this process is that often…the members of the lab propose alternate models and explanations for the unexpected findings." This results in the "use of more distant analogies. By looking at many different laboratories we also have found that when groups of scientists reason, the diversity of the group is very important. When all the scientists are from the same background it is difficult for them to generate multiple hypotheses, but when the scientists are from different backgrounds many different hypotheses can be generated."

In his *The Wisdom of Crowds*, James Surowiecki echoes the need for diversity and the value of variation. He has found there are "four conditions of smart crowds: diversity of opinion (each person should have some private information, even if it's just an eccentric interpretation of the known facts), independence (people's opinions are not determined by the opinions of those around them), decentralization (people are able to specialize and draw on local knowledge), and aggregation (some mechanism exists for turning private judgements into a collective decision)."

One of the benefits of having people from different backgrounds is that they bring with them different analogies. Dunbar reports, "Groups from the same background will draw their analogies from that background. Groups with a varied background, but with common goals, will produce many different types of analogies and these analogies can be used to solve the problem that the lab is working on. Overall, our work on distributed reasoning indicates that it is an important component of contemporary science and is frequently an aspect of scientific discovery. Furthermore, our analysis reveals that distributed reasoning can help circumvent one of the main problems in human reasoning—generating different representations and understandings of both theory and data."

Thus, teamwork reduces bias and sets the stage for insights to flourish.

It's like this

The ability of divergent groups to generate fresh analogies is incredibly important to insight generation. Analogies open the door to alternative solutions—ideas that have worked well in other situations. The scientists Dunbar studied used analogies when they got stuck. The analogies they employed were particularly effective because they understood them at a deeper structural level.

"Most research on analogy has shown that people tend to make analogies based on superficial features, rather than deep structural features. In the case of science, the scientists have both a knowledge of underlying biological mechanisms, and access to structural information….This knowledge makes it possible for the scientists to go beyond superficial characteristics in making an analogy."

This is consistent with other research by Michelene Chi and colleagues showing that effective problem solvers look to understand the deep structure of a problem by focusing on underling principles, while less effective problem solvers tend to be distracted by superficial details. A focus on underlying principles makes analogical reasoning successful.

Students who are exposed to multiple domains as part of Northwestern University's Integrated Science Program (in which they study biology, chemistry, physics, and math), according to research by Benjamin

Rottman and others, were better able to identify the underlying structures of problems. This underscores the value of diverse experience. The authors found "their multidisciplinary experience had provided them with opportunities to compare across different domains and to extract general patterns...." This is the way of the polymath, and a source of strength for Helmholtz and Poincaré.

Tetlock and Gardner point to analogy as the key to success in forecasting as well. The process for success they describe involves first identifying the underlying structure of a problem: "Unpack the question into components." And then: "Adopt the outside view and put the problem into a comparative perspective that downplays its uniqueness and treats it as a special case of a wider class of phenomena." To guard against making the problem overly abstracted and using analogies too loosely, they counsel, "Then adapt the inside view that plays up the uniqueness between your views and those of others...."

One interesting finding of Dunbar's work is that scientists use analogies more than they think. He reports, "scientists have little memory for the analogies that they use. When we go back and ask the scientists to remember how they generated a new concept or solved a problem, at a meeting that we recorded, they have little memory of how it occurred." This would suggest that analogy may play an even bigger role than is generally appreciated in the histories of innovation and insights. It is like analogy is insights' secret weapon.

Expect the unexpected

"If you do not expect the unexpected, you will not find it; for it is hard to be sought out, and difficult," Heraclitus is said to have uttered (but not in modern English), around 500 BC. The unexpected result and the anomalous finding can help us generate hypotheses that can lead to breakthroughs. "Don't discard findings that are contrary to what you expected or contrary to the conventional wisdom," says science writer Kyla Mandel. "Sometimes the unexpected can make for the best story."

Charles Darwin was always on the lookout for the unexpected. He was constantly searching for something that might cause him to revise his theories. This can be seen in his notes; for example, he makes special note of a cache of rounded stones that he found 200 feet up on cliffs overlooking the seashore. How did they get there? What did that mean about geological formation?

Recording these anomalies in his notebooks helped him, because he knew to be on guard against the tendency to forget things that didn't fit with expectations. Darwin's son Francis, writing in *The Autobiography of Charles Darwin*, explains, "There was one quality of mind which seemed to be of a special and extreme advantage in leading him to make discoveries. It was the power of never letting exceptions pass unnoticed."

These exceptions, Darwin found, helped him refine and modify his hypotheses. "I have steadfastly endeavoured to keep my mind free so as to give up any hypothesis, however much beloved (and I cannot resist forming one on every subject) as soon as facts are shown to be opposed to it....I cannot remember a single first-formed hypothesis which had not after a time to be given up or greatly modified."

Dunbar observed that in the lab single unexpected findings were often first blamed on flaws in methodology or measurement. But when the unexpected findings were replicated, or persisted despite a modification of the methodology, or there was a series of unexpected findings, things changed. "It is at this point," he reports, "that a major shift in the reasoning occurs; the scientists begin to offer new more general models, hypotheses, or theoretical explanations."

He found that scientists would often misattribute their discovery of unexpected findings to luck or chance, when in fact it was more deliberate than that. These scientists were sensitive to the unexpected and were on the lookout for it. He says, "when we analyze the strategies that scientists use in their research, we can see that they structure their research to take advantage of unexpected findings, and that they actually conduct experiments that lead to unexpected findings that they can then exploit."

"Thus," Dunbar says, "we can modify Pasteur's famous phrase of 'chance favors the prepared mind' to 'the prepared mind favors chance.'"

Mindset matters

When entering the phase of working the materials over, our mindset matters. The process is important, but so too is how we think. Philip Tetlock and his colleagues have done some quite extraordinary work on the characteristics of a good forecaster. It is remarkable because no one has done anything similar in the world of insights or intelligence analysis. We might have a feel for what makes a good researcher, but we haven't been true to our trade and researched it.

In the world of medicine, there are measures of how well doctors comply with clinical guidelines, but that just tells you what they do, and nothing about how well they do it or what mindset they bring to it. There are lots of interesting opinion pieces about what makes a good doctor, but they are just that, opinion pieces—not science.

The fact that Tetlock et al. have straightforward measures of success in forecasting uniquely allows them to dig into the qualities and mindset of what they call "superforecasters." And while forecasting is not exactly the same as generating an insight, insight is almost always needed to forecast successfully. So, before we slip into the incubation phase, let's think about our thinking.

In *Superforecasters*, Tetlock and Gardner enumerate the essential qualities of superforecasters:

"In their philosophic outlook they tend to be:
>   Cautious: Nothing is certain
>   Humble: Reality is infinitely complex
>   Nondeterministic: What happens is not meant to be and does
>   not have to happen"

This shows respect for the complexity and variability of reality. We all want simple narratives and proven procedures, but nothing about being insightful can be reduced to something so straightforward. The more we avoid oversimplifying, and the more we embrace uncertainty, the better able we are to step around the quicksand of confirmation bias and tunnel vision.

"In their abilities and thinking styles, they tend to be:

Actively open-minded: Beliefs are hypotheses to be tested, not treasures to be protected
Intelligent and knowledgeable, with a 'need for cognition': Intellectually curious, enjoy puzzles and mental challenges
Reflective: Introspective and self-critical
Numerate: Comfortable with numbers"

This open mindedness is Darwin saying, "I have steadfastly endeavoured to keep my mind free so as to give up any hypothesis, however much beloved…." The need for cognition reflects why insights professionals got into the business: they are professionally curious. Being reflective is not prejudging, as the police in Manitowoc County, Wisconsin did in Steven Avery's case. Introspection and self-criticism let people do their own peer review and take advantage of the "wisdom of the inner crowd."

"In their methods of forecasting they tend to be:
Pragmatic: Not wedded to any idea or agenda
Analytical: Capable of stepping back from the tip-of-your- nose perspective and considering other views
Dragonfly-eyed: Value diverse views and synthesize them into their own
Probabilistic: Judge using grades of maybe
Thoughtful updaters: When facts change, they change their minds."

In many respects, these methods are behavioral manifestations of their philosophies and mindsets. Pragmatism requires no set agendas, or preferred outcomes. It is being open-minded. Being analytical, dragonfly-eyed, probabilistic and open to changing your mind requires embracing complexity and uncertainty.

Check it off

Let's think about our own thinking style and ask ourselves the questions on our checklist.

BIAS DETECTION CHECKLIST	Yes	No
Did we learn from feedback from prior projects?	☐	☐
Did we get input on our preliminary thinking and ideas for insights from a diverse team?	☐	☐
Did we actively doubt our conclusions?	☐	☐
Did we actively consider and test out multiple ideas, not just our initial conclusion?	☐	☐
Do we have a broad range of evidence—including from outside our research—to support our conclusions, or are we riskily reliant on a few pieces of information?	☐	☐

If the answer to each of these questions is yes, it's time to move on to the incubation phase. You might even want to stop, turn down the lights, and take a break.

Chapter 17: Incubation

"All truly great thoughts are conceived by walking."
Friedrich Nietzsche

In a world where so much is clamoring for our time and attention, sometimes we need to step away from a problem and do something else. Einstein took frequent breaks to play his violin while he pondered a puzzle. Archimedes was in the bathtub when he suddenly realized, "Eureka! I have it!" And Sir Isaac Newton was walking through an apple orchard when the law of gravity came to him.

While doing nothing seems a paradoxical way to move forward, it does pay to step back and let your thoughts percolate—for anything from a few seconds to a few years. Not only is there an abundance of anecdotal reports, there is strong experimental evidence for the necessity of pausing and letting your thoughts incubate.

Strolling in Langley

A moment when everything comes together after a period of incubation is not unique to scientists like Einstein, Archimedes, and Newton. It happens to everyone, including intelligence analysts. "I did something else, and it was all churning around in my head, and consciously I couldn't get it to work, but when I switched over to something else, my mind kept working on it, and then something happened," said a former CIA analyst, who now teaches intelligence analysis. "People will tell you, 'I was out walking, I was in the shower, I was out back in the garden, and pow, it came to me.'"

The CIA even has an unofficial tradition of taking a walk or a run to let ideas percolate. "The Agency is in a fenced compound northwest of

Washington, and it's a large building. There's a walkway that goes around most of the building, and more by serendipity than by planning, that walk is just about a mile. A lot of people run it, and others just walk. At lunch time, or in a break between meetings, people will say, 'Let's just go out on the loop and walk,' or, 'Let's just talk, get some fresh air, get some exercise.' And those were extremely valuable things for making room for insight," the former analyst explained. "These mechanisms of taking a break, doing something different, are really valuable things to work into your life and your routine."

Rocking in Philly

Musicians, as well as analysts and scientists, see the value in letting a problem permeate your unconscious. Questlove, drummer and bandleader for The Roots, has long been interested in how to generate better ideas. In *Creative Quest* he talks about his pursuit of regularly asking other creative people for their tips. "They vary widely," he says. "Here are some, in no particular order: coffee, long walk, short walk, climb stairs, look out a window, coffee, jot down the names of everyone you know in reverse alphabetical order, meditate, listen to the radio, go to a diner and eat scrambled eggs, count to ten forward and backward, read a page of a book upside down, call a wrong number on purpose, type 'all work and no play makes Jack a dull boy' a thousand times, whittle, coffee."

Questlove even preaches the virtue of disconnecting so much that you reach a state most people will do anything to avoid: boredom. "Boredom seems like the least creative feeling," says Questlove. "It seems like a numbness. But it is actually a way of clearing space for a new idea to spring back up."

Department of Silly Walks

Comedian, actor, and writer John Cleese also believes creativity comes from unplugging from the hustle and bustle of life and allowing for some stillness. In a talk on creativity he explains, "We don't know where we get our ideas from; what we do know is that we don't get them from our laptop. In fact, we get our ideas from our unconscious, the part of our mind that goes on working when we are asleep." We also need to make space for creativity during the day. We can't just grind on and expect insights to suddenly appear. He suggests, "if you're racing around all day, ticking things off on lists, looking at your watch, making phone calls and generally just keeping all the balls in the air, you are not going to have any creative ideas."

Shirley Marland of the London North Eastern Railway also finds that "when you're running from meeting to meeting, finding creative ideas becomes more and more difficult." Her solution is to schedule an "intelligent pause to make room for ideas to unfold."

Edward Tufte is a statistician, artist, and author of excellent books on data visualization, including the classic *The Visual Display of Quantitative Information*. He too points to the need to unplug and get out: "I have stared long enough at the glowing flat rectangles of computer screen," he says. He suggests we spend more time "doing things in the real world…[such as] plant a plant, walk the dogs, read a real book, go to the opera." To facilitate that he is building a public 200+ acre tree farm and permanent exhibition place for his sculptures—a place to walk and incubate fresh ideas.

Walk it off

While there is no scientific evidence that Questlove's strategies of "read a page of a book upside down, call a wrong number on purpose, type 'all work and no play makes Jack a dull boy' a thousand times" are actually effective, there is research that proves that walking makes a difference.

"Give Your Ideas Some Legs: The Positive Effect of Walking on Creative Thinking" is a paper by Marily Oppezzo and Daniel L. Schwartz of Stanford University. In it they describe four experiments involving walking and various measures of convergent and divergent thinking, as well as analogy generation. The "experiments demonstrate that walking boosts creative ideation in real time and shortly after."

In one experiment participants were first tested sitting down, then again after walking on a treadmill. "Walking had a large effect on creativity," the authors report. "Most of the participants benefited from walking compared with sitting, and the average increase in creative output was around 60%."

In a second experiment one group of people took the creativity test twice while sitting down. The other group alternated between taking the test sitting down and then again after walking, and vice versa.

"Walking again increased people's creative production," Oppezzo and Schwartz note. "People who walked did better than those who sat, and those who only sat did not improve across trials. Walking also exhibited a residual effect on creativity. After people walked, their subsequent seated creativity was much higher than those who had not walked."

Next, participants got off the treadmill and went outside. "As before, walking—in this case, outside—led to improved creative performance," the authors write. "Also as before, walking left a residue that produced strong performance when participants were subsequently sitting." In the final experiment, they got a little creative—probably after taking a walk—and compared strolling and rolling. The fourth experiment included comparing being outside pushed around in a wheelchair versus the effects of walking outside. The wheelchair arm of the study was intended to see if simply being outdoors had an effect. It didn't.

"Walking is an easy-to-implement strategy to increase appropriate novel idea generation," Oppezzo and Schwartz suggest. "When there is a premium on generating new ideas in the workday, it should be beneficial to incorporate walks. They conclude, "many people anecdotally claim they do their best thinking when walking. We finally may be taking a step, or two, toward discovering why."

Give me a break

Walking may help because it gives us a break. It can allow the mind to focus away from the problem we've been working on and start unconscious processing.

In his book *Scatterbrain*, German neuroscientist, author, and speaker Henning Beck says, "we don't learn when we think we are learning.

We learn in the pauses *between* the thinking. Just as athletes don't improve during their training, but rather in the rest period between training sessions when they allow their bodies to adapt and heal."

"The reason for this," he suggests, "has to do with the way in which our nerve cells interact. An initial information impulse triggers a stimulus for structural changes in the cells. These changes must first be processed to prepare the cells for the next informational push. Only after they have taken a short break are they optimally prepared to react to the recurrent stimulus. If it comes too early, it will not be able to fully realize its effect. It is only by alternating information that the brain is able to imbed it in a context of related bits of knowledge."

Business culture tends to think of taking breaks as optional or even slothful. Beck believes otherwise: "The important thing is to look at breaks as part of your work, since our brain is combining ideas into possible new solutions during a supposed period of 'doing nothing.'"

Psychiatrist, brain researcher, author, and musician Srini Pillay believes a lack of focus is key to creativity. In an article entitled "Your Brain Can Only Take So Much Focus" he recommends, "The brain operates optimally when it toggles between focus and unfocus, allowing you to develop resilience, enhance creativity, and make better decisions too."

Unfocusing has an effect on the brain that can be measured. "When you unfocus, you engage a brain circuit called the 'default mode network.' Abbreviated as the DMN, we used to think of this circuit as the Do Mostly Nothing circuit because it only came on when you stopped focusing effortfully. Yet, when 'at rest,' this circuit uses 20% of the body's energy (compared to the comparatively small 5% that any effort will require).

"The DMN needs this energy because it is doing anything but resting. Under the brain's conscious radar, it activates old memories, goes back and forth between the past, present, and future, and recombines different ideas. Using this new and previously inaccessible data, you develop enhanced self-awareness and a sense of personal relevance. And you can imagine creative solutions or predict the future, thereby leading to better decision-making too."

There is evidence that sleep and dreaming facilitate incubation too.

To sleep, perchance to dream

Alexander Graham Bell, inventor of the telephone, found that sleeping on a problem helped him find solutions. He said, "I am a believer in unconscious cerebration. The brain is working all the time, though we do not know it. At night, it follows up what we think in the daytime. When I have worked a long time on one thing, I make it a point to bring all the facts regarding it together before I retire; and I have often been surprised at the results. Have you not noticed that, often, what was dark and perplexing to you the night before, is found to be perfectly solved the next morning?"

Dreams tend to have mysterious, hallucinatory properties, as random connections are made. A dreamer may report, "I was a young child flying a kite, when suddenly my boss called me back to finish my book. She was in my childhood home, fixing the car." That happens because the brain is trying out new connections, and as we near wakefulness, we become fleetingly aware of them.

"There is nothing mystical about the role of dreams in scientific discovery," says Steven Johnson. "While dream activity remains a fertile domain for research, we know that during REM sleep acetylcholine-releasing cells in the brain stem fire indiscriminately, sending surges of electricity billowing across the brain. Memories and associations are triggered in a chaotic, semi-random fashion, creating the hallucinatory quality of dreams. Most of the new neuronal connections are meaningless, but every now and then the dreaming brain stumbles across a valuable link that escaped waking consciousness."

"REM sleep is important for assimilating new information into past experience to create a richer network of associations for future use," according to research by neuroscientist Denise Cai and others. They found that "compared with quiet rest and non-REM sleep, REM enhances the integration of unassociated information for creative problem solving...."

In a chapter in *Secrets of Creativity: What Neuroscience, the Arts, and Our Minds Reveal*, Robert Stickgold explains, "The neurochemistry and neurophysiology of the brain during REM sleep is optimized for the exploration of normally ignored connections and associations within the brain's vast repertoire of stored information." During REM sleep, the brain goes wild looking for new, more remote connections. "This exploration of normally weak associations is critical to the creative process," he explains, "and REM sleep can thus be considered a period of unbridled creativity."

Others suggest slow wave sleep (SWS) plays an important role. A team out of Germany and Bulgaria led by Rolf Verledger found that "neuronal memory reprocessing during slow-wave sleep restructures task-related representations in the brain, and that such restructuring promotes the gain of explicit knowledge." In other words, SWS sleep helps us connect what we have recently learned with what we know already.

Recently, Penelope Lewis and colleagues have suggested these two mechanisms work together, like a team. "Sleep is known to be important for creative thinking, but there is a debate about which sleep stage is most relevant, and why," they write. They suggest that "rapid eye movement sleep, or 'REM,' and non-REM sleep [SWS] facilitate creativity in different ways. Memory replay mechanisms in non-REM can abstract rules from corpuses of learned information, while replay in REM may promote novel associations. We propose that the iterative interleaving of REM and non-REM across a night boosts the formation of complex knowledge frameworks, and allows these frameworks to be restructured, thus facilitating creative thought."

So, in this model, SWS and REM pass information back and forth like colleagues working on a problem together—each playing a different role. One finds analogies to things we understand well, while the other makes a more random search for new connections.

Given what we know about the power of teamwork, it's comforting to know ours brains are beavering away, trying out connections, scanning for potential insights while we sleep, all while listening to the "voice of the inner crowd."

Patience, my dear

It's brilliant that our unconscious works away while we walk, run, or sleep, but it's a process we can't control or predict. We can't even check in and see how things are going. An insight can happen in a nanosecond, when we look away from the screen, gaze at nothing, and let our unconscious pause to put two pieces of the puzzle together. Or it can take years, as we grind away at big problems. Either way, we struggle to glimpse what is going on behind the curtain.

Gary Klein, in *Seeing What Others Don't,* calls these incubating thoughts "fragile creatures, easily lost to the more pressing needs of day-to-day issues." Tom McLeish, in *The Poetry and Music of Science,* likens our unconscious ruminations to an apprehensive wild animal. "But like all shy creatures," he says, "we tend to detect its movements only in the periphery of our vision. When we turn to stare at it full on, the experience of unconscious ideation is apparently nowhere to be seen."

And so, we linger in the dark, quietly—lest we scare off the insight— and impatiently. We yearn to progress to the next stage, the Eureka! moment. But we must wait.

Sweet dreams.

Chapter 18: The insight surfaces

"Eureka, I have found it!"
Archimedes

The haunting call of the loon reverberating around the lake is a highlight of summer evenings at the family cottage. With their long elegant necks, the regal black and white patterning on their feathers, and their graceful gliding in the water, these beautiful birds bring a certain grace to the lake.

During the day, a favorite pastime is to watch the loons while they hunt for fish. They'll be silently padding along when they suddenly disappear underwater and start swimming, propelled by webbed feet and incredibly powerful wings. These astonishing birds can dive down as far as 250 feet and stay underwater for up to five minutes.

With us watching from the dock, a loon might swim up-close, give us a quizzical glance, and then suddenly dive down, only to burst to the surface minutes later—halfway across the lake. Or they might lunge under the canoe and pop up on the other side, just seconds after. Their unpredictability makes them a perfect lazy day pleasure.

Insights are like loons. You never know where or when they will surface, but when they do, they'll make a splash.

Splish splash, I was taking a bath

Eureka entered our language because of some clever detective work. Hiero of Syracuse, circa 250 BC, had commissioned a votive crown for the local temple. But he suspected his goldsmith was pocketing some of the gold. The crown weighed exactly what it was supposed to, but Hiero could not shake the feeling he was being conned. So, he asked Archimedes—who was known around Syracuse as a pretty bright guy—to figure out if his suspicion was justified.

Archimedes gathered information, worked it over in his mind, and, having no luck, thought he'd take a bath and mull it over. As he stepped into the bath, he noticed the water level rose in equal volume to the volume of his legs. He realized he could now measure the crown's volume and weight and could thus calculate its density. Since gold is considerably denser than other metals, he was able to determine if the goldsmith was inserting cheaper metals into the crown.

His insight was sudden, certain and exciting. It was so thrilling that Archimedes jumped out the bath and dashed naked through the streets of Syracuse, shouting "Eureka! I have found it" as he rushed to share his news. The jig was up for the thieving goldsmith, and Archimedes would be a hero to Hiero.

The anatomy of Eureka!

A eureka or aha moment tends to have four characteristics: suddenness, ease of appearance, a positive feeling, and a sense of confidence in the result. How intense these feelings are is linked to how dramatic the insight is. An idea about how to solve a simple problem will often appear suddenly and easily and seem right or true. That feels good. But it probably won't have you running naked through the streets. Nonetheless, the structure of this insight is the same as Archimedes's eureka moment.

Bruce Grierson sums it up nicely: "To the brain…an epiphany about existence may not be categorically different from the sudden insight that you can tell the freshness of a loaf of supermarket bread by the color of the bag-tag." Let's unpack these four qualities of a moment of insight.

Suddenness reflects a transfer of the insight from the unconscious to the conscious mind. Kounios and Beeman, measuring the brain when an insight emerges, observe a "brain blink" that precedes sudden awareness of the solution. It is a burst of alpha waves followed by a surge of gamma waves. This is the signal of a thought emerging from the deep darkness of the unconscious into the bold light of day.

This sense of suddenness is confirmed in a classic study by Janet Metcalfe and David Wiebe. They presented people with sets of both insight and analytic problems and asked them to estimate relatively how long it would take to solve each set of problems. They found "the data indicated that noninsight problems were open to accurate predictions of performance, whereas insight problems were opaque to such predictions." You can't tell when an insight will emerge, but, when using analytical reasoning, you can effectively estimate when you are getting close to a solution.

While people were working on the problems, the authors also asked them, every fifteen seconds, how close they were to a solution. That confirmed "that insight problems are…solved by a sudden flash of illumination; noninsight problems are solved more incrementally."

Ease is apparent when what had been a seemingly intractable problem becomes effortless. Sascha Topolinski and Rolf Reber, in their paper "Gaining Insight into the Aha! Experience," suggest this sudden ease "increases positive affect, the judged truth of the solution (independent of its actual truth), and subjective confidence in this truth judgment." In other words, the itch has been scratched and it feels good. And the thought appears complete and true, because it was easy.

Barbara McClintock was a Nobel Prize-winning geneticist supervising a postdoc studying the exchange of genetic material in corn. In one experiment, the researcher expected half of the plant's pollen would be normal and half would be sterile. Instead, he discovered that only 25-30 percent of the pollen was sterile. He and McClintock were surprised by this, and she retreated from the field to her lab to ponder its meaning. After thinking it over for a little while she suddenly "jumped up and ran down to the field" shouting "Eureka! I have it! I have the answer!" Genes normally come in pairs, but she suddenly realized this outcome was due to an extra, unexpected, third copy of the gene.

She excitedly blurted out her insight, but her colleagues met her with: "How does that work?" At first, she did not know. But she was certain. "It had all been done fast," she said. "The answer came, and I'd run [to the corn field]. Now I worked it out, step by step—it was an intricate set of steps—and I came out with what it was….Something happens," she explained, "that you have the answer—before you are able to put it into words. It is all done subconsciously. This has happened too many times to me, and I know when to take it seriously. I am so absolutely certain."

Dream it up

Acetylcholine is a chemical that facilitates the transfer of nerve signals, and its release in the brain is significantly greater during REM sleep— when dreams occur. Amazingly, the discovery that acetylcholine transfers nerve signals in the brain came in a dream. But the insight was almost lost because the discoverer wrote it down illegibly.

Otto Loewi was a German-born physician, pharmacologist, and psychobiologist who won a Nobel Prize for his discovery that acetylcholine is a neurotransmitter. He had the idea that nerve signals were possibly transmitted using chemical instructions. But, for years, he could not prove it.

One night—17 years after he first started thinking about it—the answer came to him in a dream. He woke up, scribbled down his insight and fell back asleep. When he awoke the next day, he didn't remember the solution, and he could not read what he has scrawled down in his half-dreaming state. After 17 years—that's a long loon dive—he was crushed.

Fortunately, the next night the dream came again. This time he woke himself up enough to write it down legibly.

Professor André Lachaîne was not so lucky.

Write it down

André Lachaîne was a professor of physics, a musician, and a raconteur who described himself as a Licensed Quantum Mechanic. He was also a friend and musical collaborator. André recorded a sad tale of lost insights with Austin Lowe, Greg Forbes, Michael Hurley, and myself entitled "I shoulda wrote it down!" In it he wryly improvised:

> "I had a dream. A perfect dream.
> Everything was revealed to me—the whole universe…
>
> Everything was so simple. Revelation.
> Diaphanous. Beautiful…
>
> Revealed, all the mysteries.
> I was in awe and wonderment.
>
> It's so simple. I shouldn't write it down.
> It's so simple, I'll remember it tomorrow morning, no
> problem…
>
> The alpha of it all was revealed.
> The beta, the beta of Buddha.
>
> The gamma of God, the delta, the epsilon.
> It was all there…
>
> The omega, the psi.
> The sigh of psi…
>
> It was all there. So simple.
> I didn't have to wake myself up and write it down…
>
> It was so simple. Why didn't I write it down?
> Christ! Why didn't I write it down!?"

Graffiti it

One person who did write it down, who literally carved his insight into a bridge, was William Rowan Hamilton—a noted Irish mathematician and astronomer. On October 16th, 1843, Hamilton was walking along the banks of the Royal Canal, when suddenly the answer to a problem he had been puzzling over came to him. He quickly scratched his formula for Quaternion algebra into the bridge: $i^2 = j^2 = k^2 = ijk = -1$. Quaternions describe mechanics in three-dimensional space, and his insight would later be key in many technological developments, including sending men to the moon and developing computer-generated 3D imagery in games and movies.

In a letter to his son, he described the moment: "An electric circuit seemed to close; and a spark flashed forth the herald (as I foresaw immediately) of many long years to come of definitely directed thought and work...." Here we again see the gathering of information, a working over of the problem, and a long incubation, followed by a sudden insight, the easy-feeling solution, and a sense of full understanding. He was not going to let this hard-fought-for idea slip away.

"Nor could I resist the impulse...to cut with a knife on a stone of Brougham Bridge, as we passed it, the fundamental formula which contains the Solution of the Problem...." Here we have, in 1843 Dublin, probably not the first, and certainly not the last, insight graffiti.

Unlike André, he not only wrote it down, he inscribed it. A monument to his insight stands on the bridge to this day.

Insights investigated

I am not sure André truly had the answer for "everything" in his dream. Not all revelations that are sudden, easy, and feel certain end up being right.

Margaret Webb and colleagues have, however, found that "feelings of insight were reported for correct and incorrect solutions, but the feeling of insight was stronger for correct solutions." Similarly, an investigation by Amory Danek and Jennifer Wiley found "major quantitative differences between Aha! experiences that follow correct and incorrect solutions....Compared to incorrect, correct solutions were rated as more pleasant and more sudden and solvers were more confident about being correct."

These are promising indications that what feels like an insight probably is one, but fresh ideas benefit from being tested, tweaked, and retested. And when they are proven, they need to be communicated effectively.

That brings us to the last stage of insight generation. As Webb described it, this is "the final shaping and development of the idea to practical usefulness."

Chapter 19: Idea, meet reality

"Certitude is not the test of certainty. We have been cocksure of many things that were not so."
Oliver Wendell Holmes

You've gathered information, worked it over in your mind, let it incubate for a while, and had an idea surface. Now comes the time to take that insight and reality check it, refine it, and figure out how to communicate it in a way that makes clear the "so what?" and "what's next?"

"In this stage," James Webb Young says, "you have to take your little new-born idea out into the world of reality. And when you do you usually find it is not quite the marvelous child it seemed when you first gave birth to it...."

"Do not make the mistake of holding the idea close to your chest. Submit it to the criticism of the judicious.

"When you do, a surprising thing will happen. You will find that a good idea has, as it were, self-expanding qualities. It stimulates those who see it to add to it. Thus possibilities in it which you have overlooked will come to light."

This stage has two parts. The first is obtaining feedback on your idea. The second is communicating it effectively. Let's start with bringing your baby out to meet the world.

Back to the future

Now we return to where we started. We need to think critically. Our unconscious has been working overtime, and this is the moment for our conscious mind to pull its weight.

We know we are pattern-detecting machines, and that while that is a great strength, it is also a weakness. It can lead us to confirmation bias or tunnel vision or any manner of reality-blurring bias. Teamwork, in the form of peer review and feedback, is invaluable. Others can see what you missed. They can spot holes in your logic, faulty assumptions in your analysis, and implications you have not yet considered. Here is where doubt shines a spotlight on your new-born idea and gazes upon it with an arched eyebrow.

The checklist comes in handy again at this stage, as a process test. Did we learn from prior research? Did we get input on our preliminary thinking and ideas for insights from a diverse team? Are we actively doubting our conclusions? Have we considered and tested out multiple ideas, not just our initial conclusion? Do we have a broad range of evidence—including from outside our research—to support our conclusions, or are we riskily reliant on a few pieces of information?

These are all uncomfortable questions. They can chafe after you've just had an aha moment. But if we are 100% certain our insight is correct, we are most certainly wrong.

There is no idea or insight that cannot be improved.

Testing, testing, 1,2,3

"The notion of the empiric method is based upon the simple premise of trial and error," writes Robert Burton in *On Being Certain*. "With crossword puzzles, you don't expect all your first choices to be the final ones. Ditto for working our equations for tough math problems, designing your home, or writing a symphony. The history of science is the history of successive approximations."

"My general approach is to say, 'Here's what we believe, and here's why we believe it,'" Rogers Media's Greg Dinsmore told me. "It's implicitly testing a bunch of assumptions. You test alternative hypotheses to see if the conclusion you're coming to makes sense."

This showing of how you got to your insight is a balancing act. Show too much and you lose people. But show too little and you miss the opportunity for people to provide constructive feedback. Without some understanding of how we came to our conclusions, people are not equipped to question our evidence and assumptions.

"I think there's a value in taking people through the reasoning that gets you to the conclusion," Dinsmore says. "People will challenge it, but that's the point. That's one of the ways of getting around the biases. You can't show all your work because, at some point, there are a whole pile of judgement calls to be made. But, as a rule, you want to say, 'Okay, we came to this conclusion. It was because we asked this question, and it produced this result, and then we have this other data point over here that gives us further confidence that the answer is accurate.'"

You've probably been on your insight journey for some time. You know the work you put in to end up where you're at. But others have not been on the same journey, so it's important that they get up to speed quickly and accurately. That means you need to communicate your insight efficiently and effectively. More on that, after we think about how people might respond to your insight.

Feedback can be overwhelming

It's essential to be open to people's critiques of your insights. But it's also vitally important to not accept every comment as completely valid. People tend to be suspicious of new insights. If it challenges their expectations, an insight can trigger negative reactions, simply because it fails to confirm their biases.

"I suppose the process of acceptance will pass through the usual four stages," suggests geneticist J.B.S. Haldane:

"1. This is worthless nonsense,
2. This is an interesting, but perverse, point of view,
3. This is true, but quite unimportant,
4. I always said so."

Thomas Khun, in his *The Structure of Scientific Revolutions*, notes that real advancement in understanding is always a struggle. "In science," he writes, "novelty emerges only with difficulty, manifested by resistance, against a background provided by expectation."

Even the serendipitous discovery of X-rays was not universally acclaimed at first. "X-rays…were greeted not only with surprise but with shock," Kuhn said. "Lord Kelvin at first pronounced them as an elaborate hoax."

Jennifer Mueller and colleagues have done some intriguing research on people's innate bias against new ideas. In their paper "The Bias Against Creativity: Why People Desire But Reject Creative Ideas," they found that while people indicate they desire creativity, implicit association testing revealed that people "associate creativity with uncertainty, failure, and lack of practicality….Furthermore, the bias against creativity interfered with participants' ability to recognize a creative idea."

So, don't expect your brilliant insight to always receive an immediately warm reception. Listen and learn and be prepared to explain.

Ahead of his time

Ignaz Semmelweis was a Hungarian physician who specialized in obstetrics. In 1846 he was appointed to the Allgemeine Krankenhaus— the Vienna General Hospital— which was renowned for its meticulous record keeping and analysis. Semmelweis, among his other duties, was responsible for maintaining the records on his ward. He was keenly aware that 10% of the women who passed through that ward died of childbirth fever. No one knew why.

Possible reasons people floated for this terrible death rate included catching chills, fear, bad diet, embarrassment, and getting up too soon after giving birth. Semmelweis's boss, Professor Klein, was fairly sure the deaths were due to some sort of malodourous scent or miasma in the air. But nobody was certain, and the existence of germs and bacteria had not yet been discovered.

This Viennese institution was a teaching hospital, and Semmelweis's ward was manned by doctors and medical students. There was another obstetrical ward, staffed by midwives and those training in midwifery. The death rate on the ward run by midwives was just 3%. Semmelweis noted this and took it on as his mission to understand the cause of the fatal fever and how he might prevent it.

One thing that stood out to him was that deaths would often come in clusters. In some months, the death rate soared as high as 30%. In other cases, women whose beds were in a row would all become infected. Often the newborns of the infected women would also develop the fever and die. Semmelweis puzzled over this.

Pathology had, in recent years, become as an important source of learning for physicians. Autopsies were performed on the dead mothers, and there was no shortage of them. In addition to confirming the nature of the disease, the autopsy was used to train the younger doctors in anatomy. When they cut open these unfortunate young women, they were invariably oozing pus and other foul liquids. The doctors would perform these autopsies and then head to the ward to deliver babies, often without washing their hands. But no one thought anything of it.

Then one of Semmelweis's mentors died, after being nicked with a scalpel during an autopsy. He too developed a fever and perished. Suddenly, Semmelweis understood.

Awful insight

He writes, "Totally shattered, I brooded over the case with intense emotion until suddenly a thought crossed my mind; at once it became clear that childbed fever, the fatal sickness of the newborn and the disease of Professor Kolletshka were one and the same because they all consist pathologically of the same anatomic changes. If, therefore, in the case of Professor Kolletshka general sepsis [contamination of the blood] arose from the inculcation of cadaver particles, then [childbirth] fever must originate from the same source."

Now it was obvious to Semmelweis why there was such a difference in mortality between the physician-run ward and the one operated by midwives. The midwives were not doing autopsies and then seeing patients; only the physicians were.

Surgeon Sherwin Nuland, in his biography of Semmelweis, *The Doctor's Plague,* writes, "In a single insight Semmelweis had solved both parts of the problem he has set for himself—to identify the nature of [childbirth] fever and how to prevent it." Semmelweis reasoned that a chloride solution would be the ideal substance to destroy the foul-smelling cadaver particles. Nuland says Semmelweis "insisted every entering medical attendant wash in it before touching a woman in labor." The death rate dropped to just 3%.

"Other than the practice of chlorine hand cleaning, only one other change had been made," Nuland says. "[Semmelweis's boss] Klein convinced himself that a recently installed ventilation system was the reason for the startingly improved statistics. It was the only way he could rationalize the fact staring him in the face, and he clung to it as to an amulet."

Selling the story

Now Semmelweis just had to convince others of his insight. This, unfortunately, proved difficult. Semmelweis failed to effectively communicate his proof. He did no experiments, he wrote no papers, and he failed to use an emerging new technology—the microscope—to further explore the problem. He thought there was no point because, for him, the clinical evidence was enough.

Semmelweis was also gravely moved by the realization of what he'd been doing. He said, "God only knows the number of patients who have gone to their graves prematurely by my fault." The same was true for the other obstetricians. Reflecting on this, Nuland asks, "What must it have been like, to be confronted by a theory that placed the blame for hundreds of deaths squarely on the shoulders of the very obstetricians who were being asked to evaluate its validity in an objective manner? For many it would prove to be intolerable. Better to convince oneself that it could not be true, as Klein seemed to be doing."

When people did not adopt his methods, Semmelweis, rather than provide a better explanation, became defensive and angry. He was adamant that the clinical record spoke for itself and he saw no need to further elaborate. Others felt differently. Tensions rose.

At the end of Semmelweis's two-year term, Klein refused to renew his contract. Semmelweis "appealed to the dean's office, but Klein countered by accusing him of autocratic behavior in the way he kept demanding that students and staff wash in the chlorine solution." With Semmelweis gone, the hospital stopped using the handwashing procedure, and the death rate rose again. Semmelweis was enraged by this and the failure to adopt his methods in other hospitals.

Nuland says, "Always intolerant of disagreement, [Semmelweis] indulged himself in outbursts of anger that grew more explosive with each incident. He gave increasing free rein to a rapierlike sarcasm with which he skewered opponents and obstructionists. Semmelweis become more and more unpopular. And he did not care."

Fourteen years after his sudden insight, Semmelweis finally decided to write *The Etiology, the Concept, and the Prophylaxis of Childhood Fever,* in order to explain his ideas. Nuland says it "is a complex book, written in a complex manner by a complex man....The result is 543 pages of a book that is logorrheic, repetitious, hectoring, accusatory, self-glorifying, sometimes confused, tedious, detailed to the point of aridity—in sum, virtually unreadable."

Nuland says, "So deeply absorbed was he in the scientific validity and even the moral righteousness of his teachings that he was oblivious to the daunting problem facing anyone making a serious attempt to follow the arguments he was presenting." In *The Etiology,* Nuland says, "Semmelweis goes much further than justifying his doctrines; he never hesitates to level charges against some of the most prominent obstetricians of the time, calling them ignoramuses for not subscribing to his teachings. And worse yet—they are accused of being unrepentant murderers of the women whose lives have been entrusted to them."

Semmelweis grew increasingly out of control. Eventually, he became so dysfunctional his friends and family tricked him into entering an asylum. There, things got worse. Semmelweis's wife said, "my husband had tried to get out and, when he was forcibly restrained, fell into a fit of delirium so that six attendants could scarcely hold him back." While being restrained he was badly beaten. Two weeks later he was dead.

The autopsy revealed that wounds he suffered in the melee became infected, and it spread to his blood. Semmelweis died of the same disease he had devoted his life to preventing.

Semmelweis's tragic downward spiral occurred because he failed to effectively communicate his insights and was therefore unable to convince people of their importance. Once better explained, his insights saved millions of lives.

Let's not make the same mistake. We must communicate effectively.

Chapter 20: Communicating insights effectively

"Insights don't count for much if we can't translate them into action."
Gary Klein

In order to turn insights into action, people need to understand the "So what?" and "Why does it matter?" The answer to these questions must be communicated in a clear and concise manner, with just the right amount of supporting evidence. The effect can be transformational.

Maria Popova writes, "A great storyteller—whether a journalist or editor or filmmaker or curator [or insights professional]—helps people figure out not only what matters in the world, but also why it matters. A great storyteller dances up the ladder of understanding, from information to knowledge to wisdom. Through symbol, metaphor, and association, the storyteller helps us interpret information, integrate it with our existing knowledge, and transmute that into wisdom…. At a time when information is increasingly cheap and wisdom increasingly expensive, this gap is where the modern storyteller's value lives."

Focus on the audience

For a story to be effective, it needs to reach the audience where they are. *Nature* suggests, "Effective communication…is centered on the audience: It is audience-friendly, just as effective software is user-friendly. In your communication, focus on what your audience needs or wants to learn, not on what you feel like telling them. Strive to see things from their perspective. Keep in mind all the potential members of your audience…not just those who have expertise or interests similar to your own."

Dr. Arvi Grover, the cardiologist, finds that understanding where his patients are at is essential in explaining to them what they need to do to improve their heart health. "I try to understand what level of understanding they are at," he told me. "Then I tell them a story with a beginning, a body and an end. I try to impress upon them how they can improve their lives. You have to teach them in a way that is conducive to change. I try to explain how change can have a positive impact. Rather than try to scare them, I try to motivate them."

I asked Kyla Mandel, a science writer, how she sells her story ideas to harried and jaded editors. She explains, "The best pitches need to grab your attention immediately, spark your curiosity, and tell you clearly and concisely what the 'new' thing is, why it's different than other stories, and why it matters, in a way that leaves you wanting more but doesn't leave you confused as to what the story is."

She believes it is important to be concise. Her suggestion: "Try writing your pitch in one sentence on a piece of paper. And then refine it, and refine it again. And then use this as the hook to grab someone's attention."

Brevity is so important to the United States Army they made it a regulation.

Be concise

BLUF is the Army's acronym for "bottom line up front." You can find it in Army Regulation 25-50 by order of General Raymond T. Odierno, United States Army Chief of Staff. "In accordance with Public Law (PL) 111–274…[Army] writing will be clear, concise, and effective. Army correspondence must aid effective communication and decision making.

"Effective Army writing is understood by the reader in a single rapid reading and is free of errors in substance, organization, style, and correctness….Two essential requirements include putting the main point at the beginning of the correspondence (bottom line up front) and using the active voice."

Author, filmmaker, and activist Susan Sontag approaches the need to be selective a little more poetically. She says, "Every writer…wants to tell many stories, but we know that we can't tell all the stories — certainly not simultaneously. We know we must pick one story, well, one central story; we have to be selective."

"Creativity is subtraction," says Austin Kleon in his *Steal Like an Artist*. He feels that "In this age of information abundance and overload, those who will get ahead will be the folks who figure out what to leave out, so they can concentrate on what's really important…."

Dr. Seuss believed in economy of vocabulary, as well as being concise. He wrote *The Cat in the Hat* with just 236 different words. On a bet with his editor, he later penned *Green Eggs and Ham* with just 50 different words. Brilliant.

Let's leave the last word on economy of language to George Orwell: "I think the following rules will cover most cases:

> i. Never use a metaphor, simile, or other figure of speech which you are used to seeing in print.
> ii. Never use a long word where a short one will do.
> iii. If it is possible to cut a word out, always cut it out.
> iv. Never use the passive where you can use the active.
> v. Never use a foreign phrase, a scientific word, or a jargon word if you can think of an everyday English equivalent.
> vi. Break any of these rules sooner than say anything outright barbarous."

The pause that refreshes

In the age of Twitter and rapid response, there can be a sense of urgency to share an insight immediately. But insights are like fruit: if you wait and let them ripen a little, they can be even better. Notre Dame Professor Emeritus Mark Noll is an advocate for pausing and pondering before posting. As an historian, he understands the importance of context and how time can provide a perspective that enriches your understanding. He feels, "if you're working on topics that require not just diving deep but trying to get context, it's almost impossible to work rapidly." Noll advocates stepping back from your conclusions, if only overnight. To illustrate the value of this, he told me about an exhibition of letters that U.S. President Abraham Lincoln signed, but decided not to post.

"There was a wonderful exhibit in DC, maybe 10 years ago. It was a display, at the National Archives, of autographed letters of Abraham Lincoln that he'd never sent. He had a practice of waiting a day or two after he wrote a letter to post it. There is a surprising number that he just never sent." Lincoln had written and signed these letters, but waited and reread them. Then he revised his thoughts. This exhibit underscored, for Noll, the value of stepping back, reconsidering your thoughts, and sharpening your narrative.

En pointe communication

London North Eastern Railway (LNER) runs from London up to Leeds and beyond, going as far north as Inverness, Scotland. LNER recently upgraded from older high-speed trains to brand new Azuma trains, which are based on Japanese bullet train technology. Shirley Marland was the Customer Experience Manager, and she led a team of "Azuma Pioneers." They were from across the business and were charged with leading changeover and the creation of the processes required for the new fleet. She likes to use analogies and metaphors to help ensure a "message has landed well, that it will be remembered." She likes to "tell a story that people feel a connection with, and then apply it to the message you want to get across."

At a recent conference, where she was speaking about the experience of building the Azuma Pioneer team, she used ballet as her hook from her first slide onward. "At the end of the presentation," she recounted, "I got everyone to stand up and we went through a summary of the key messages using ballet positions.

"Standing with my arms in first position represented making sure I really prepared: that I knew what my objectives were. And as I rose, I gathered my arms up into second position. That was gathering my stakeholders and making sure the entire business was on board.

"Opening my arms into third position was opening up the opportunity for the group of pioneers to come on their journey with me. Then I was gathering my arm into fourth position, which was taking the people on the journey of figuring out what we were going to deliver as a customer experience on board these trains. And then my other arm came up into fifth position.

"With both arms overhead we're at the top, and all these elements have come together. And at this point we're taking the project up to a next level, so I rose up on the balls of my feet into fifth position, relevé. And then I brought the arms down back into first place, reflecting on the project, reflecting on lessons learned. It was using those movements to summarize the story. And a nice little curtsy at the end to say thank you very much." That's a memorable way to convey an insight, though I doubt it would meet army regulations.

Possibly precise

The words we use matter. Unintentionally vague statements can be read in many ways, allowing the reader to interpret them whatever way makes sense to them. Unfortunately, people do this without being aware they are potentially missing the point. Bertram Forer demonstrated this in 1948 with an exquisitely simple experiment in his psychology class.

One week he had the students complete a personality test, telling them that he would analyze the results and generate a personality report for each of them. He handed back the results the following class, with each report bearing the student's name. Students were seated so that they could not see others' reports, under the pretext that they were going to have a quiz later in class.

The students were asked to read their report and rate it on how well they felt it captured their personality. They obviously felt the reports were pretty spot-on, giving them an average accuracy rating of 4.2 out of 5. There was just one wrinkle: all of the reports were identical. All the students were given the exact same personality profile.

The report was based on vague phrases clipped from a newsstand astrology book. The profiles included the statement "You pride yourself as an independent thinker and do not accept others' statements without satisfactory proof."

The language we choose to explain our insights matters, particularly when it comes to conveying our level of certainty.

Yugoslavia was one country

Sherman Kent was the founder of the CIA's Office of National Estimates (ONE). He aimed for precision in the team's estimates and was appalled when he discovered just how varied people's interpretations of the language of their estimates could be. He believed, given that their estimates were going to the President, the Cabinet and the Chiefs of Staff, that they "should set forth the community's findings in such a way as to make clear to the reader what is certain knowledge and what is reasoned judgment, and within this large realm of judgment what varying degrees of certitude lie behind each key statement." That's laudable, given how crucial their communications were.

It was 1951 when Kent realized how difficult it was to achieve the clarity he was aiming for. ONE was producing an estimate, now unclassified, entitled "Probability of an Invasion of Yugoslavia in 1951." Yugoslavia, at the time, was Communist but defiantly not part of the Soviet Union. The key conclusion of the estimate was: "we believe that the extent of Satellite military and propaganda preparations indicates that an attack on Yugoslavia in 1951 should be considered a serious possibility."

What would you conclude the probability of an attack was from this statement? What percent chance would you estimate?

Kent writes, "A few days after the estimate appeared, I was in informal conversation with the Policy Planning Staff's chairman. We spoke of Yugoslavia and the estimate. Suddenly he said, 'By the way, what did you people mean by the expression "serious possibility"? What kind of odds did you have in mind?' I told him that my personal estimate was on the dark side, namely, that the odds were around 65 to 35 in favor of an attack. He was somewhat jolted by this; he and his colleagues had read 'serious possibility' to mean odds very considerably lower. Understandably troubled by this want of communication, I began asking my own colleagues on the Board of National Estimates what odds they had had in mind when they agreed to that wording. It was another jolt to find that each Board member had had somewhat different odds in mind and the low man was thinking of about 20 to 80, the high of 80 to 20. The rest ranged in between."

Thus, Sherman Kent's endeavor to define what he called "words of estimative probability" was born. He and a colleague started with a set of 11 words which they linked to ranges of numeric probabilities. "At once we perceived our folly," he said. "In the first place, given the inexactness of the intelligence data we were working with, the distinctions we made between one set of odds and its fellows above and below were unjustifiably sharp. And second, even if in rare cases one could arrive at such exact mathematical odds, the verbal equivalent could not possibly convey that exactness. The laudable precision would be lost on the reader."

Even after he moved to a shorter scale, he struggled to have it obtain widespread adoption within the CIA. There was an ongoing scuffle between what he called the "poets" and the "mathematicians." Alan Barnes, in Canada, nailed down the communication of probabilities in his Middle East and Africa intelligence division over 50 years later by testing alternative wordings and measuring how they were perceived. He was able to produce estimates that were remarkably right and correctly understood. Like Kent, Mandel, and Tetlock, Barnes sided with the mathematicians.

As insights professionals, we usually don't deal with forecasting probabilities. But we can learn from these examples that communication can be maddeningly vague, and that we need to pay close attention to the words we use.

Tell me what you learned

In communicating insights, it is critical to have the audience provide you with feedback. This not only helps you combat biases; it also opens you up to new information your stakeholders might possess. This additional knowledge aids the evolution of your insights.

The cycle of insight development continues, ever iterating, growing larger, in a fractal pattern. We gather information, we process it, we let it incubate, the insights emerge, and we test them out—aiming to communicate in way that is concise and precise.

Thankfully, insights never stop arising.

Conclusion: The ongoing journey to insight

"There is nothing so terrible as activity without insight."
Johann Wolfgang von Goethe

Early on I said, "This book is about insights. It starts with looking at how we learn and how we make connections. It then moves on to look at how biases—cognitive and otherwise—can limit our insights or lead us astray. Next it examines strategies that can help us avoid or mitigate those biases. The final portion shines a light on the process of generating insights, exploring ways we can improve and enhance them." We have come to the end of that journey and now is the moment to briefly retrace our steps, so that we can see the pattern afresh.

Predictably unpredictable

Insights are tricky because, while there is a definite process for generating them, it is not precisely predictable. The workings of our brains present a double-edged sword. Our thinking can reveal connections that lead the world to see things in a whole new light. But we can also make the wrong associations and end up providing misleading conclusions.

Our natural proclivity to see patterns and to quickly fill in the blanks can lead us to leap to the wrong conclusion, in a way that feels perfectly natural and "makes sense." Confirmation bias, tunnel vision, WYSIATI, and hindsight bias all bedevil our attempts to generate accurate insights.

We need to be conscious of these biases, but awareness is not enough. Because we are blind to our own preconceptions, we are also oblivious to their pernicious effects. That's where teamwork comes in. We can see other people's biases and they can see ours. But that's only helpful if we ensure we make the effort to share our thoughts and ideas and get feedback.

As an industry, we need to make more space for teamwork. We must further strengthen our processes for sharing and make sure we reward team efforts. It is easy to identify and compensate individual achievements, but recognizing the impact of teams sharing ideas is more of a challenge. It is, however, a challenge we must rise to.

In medicine, we see thousands of deaths each year because of unchecked biases. In law, we see hundreds of wrongful convictions due to biases that go undetected. The impact we observe with these fellow sense-makers serves as a graphic reminder of the very real impact of biases. The effect of biases on our insights is no less real.

Coupled with teamwork, doubt can be a tool to neutralize bias. Not endless gnawing self-doubt, but a willingness to question everything. Is there something we missed? Is there a dog that did not bark? Is an unexpected finding the key to unlocking a deeper understanding?

Checklists and other structured analytic techniques can also remind us to consider alternatives and not just settle for a conclusion that is easy and makes sense. But the work of David Mandel and the history of ACH reminds us we must test these methods and not just assume they are effective.

Inexplicable insights

Insights are mysterious, bordering on the miraculous. The fact that our unconscious mind churns away, looking for new connections while we eat, walk, and sleep, is astounding. And that connection-seeking process continues, invisible to us, sometimes for years. But our unconscious mind can only work with what we put into it. It's like a great meal. If we don't start with the best ingredients, we'll never get transcendent results.

The more sources we imbibe, and the more varied they are, the greater the originality and incisiveness of our insights. When we get to the stage of working a problem out in our minds, teamwork is, again, a powerful resource. And, like the information we take in, having input from people with diverse perspectives, or even dissenting opinions, is critically important. Tetlock's ground-breaking work reveals that our mindset needs to be cautious, humble, reflective, and actively openminded. Then we go for a walk, or take a nap, and let our unconscious mind do its work.

Insights are like acorns. On their own they are not much. But planted in the minds of others, and nurtured effectively, they can grow to become mighty oaks. When the idea, insight, or innovation does surface, the tragic story of Dr. Semmelweis reminds us of the importance of communicating our insights effectively. Follow U.S. Army regulation 25-50: bottom line up front.

I hope this look at how ideas, insights, and innovations are generated helps spur your own insights about insights. We've learned from a diverse set of sense-makers how they face this challenge. Now is the time to put the book down and let your mind start making new connections. Happy eureka!

Acknowledgements

I'd like to thank Ged Parton, CEO of Maru Group, for encouraging me to write this book, granting me free rein, and ensuring I had time to research and write. It's been a privilege and a pleasure for which am truly grateful. Thanks also to clients and colleagues, past and present, for enriching my understanding of the power of insights.

Interviews with David Mandel, Greg Dinsmore, Scarlett Janusas, Mark Noll, Sam Reimer, Kyla Mandel, Ciara O'Connell, and Shirley Marland were very helpful and are much appreciated. A special thank you to a NYPD detective, and a former CIA-analyst who now is a professor of intelligence analysis. These two agreed to be interviewed despite having to do so anonymously. Your willingness to help is valued.

My love, Yola Zdanowicz, has been incredibly encouraging and understanding. She just smiles patiently (or maybe rolls her eyes) when, in the middle of doing something, I stop, stare off into space and then silently nod as an insight comes and I scramble to make a note. Thanks also to my sons Cameron, Colin and Ian. They pleasantly endured me burbling on at dinner about things like obscure biases, the CIA and the importance of handwashing after performing autopsies.

I've long been interested in cross-disciplinary learning and the power of combinatorial creativity, but two of my family members provided inputs that helped generate the idea for this book. My brother John's wife, Sue Bazley, is an archeologist. We were together at my sister Cathy's camp just as I was finishing *The Insights Revolution: Questioning Everything*. Sue read a draft and remarked at the many parallels between the insights industry and archeological research. That really struck me, and started me thinking about what we can learn from other disciplines.

My brother Bruce curated an incredible exhibition at the Vancouver Art Gallery in 2016 called *MashUp: The Birth of Modern Culture*. It was an exciting and inspiring look at the history of combinatorial creativity in everything from collage, to sampling, to film, to writing, to sculpture, and more. The show's cross-disciplinary and boundary-smashing approach resulted in an exhibition and book of wonderful diversity and richness. I was inspired by this testament to the incredible power of combinational creativity.

Thank you, Sue and Bruce.

Grant Heckman has again been a wonderful editor. Working with him is like watching a magician. I know what he's doing, but I don't understand how he does it. I stand in awe of his sleuthing skills, his focus, and his ability to bring peace to tortured phrases. Any remaining mistakes are mine.

Michael Cusden, in a myriad of ways, has played a huge role in getting this book into your hands. Thanks for your support, encouragement and wry humor. I really appreciate it.

Thanks also to Megan Paul for her help and good cheer. A special shout-out to Megan's new baby boy Jackson. His gestation and birth paralleled that of this book almost exactly. I wish him all the best in his insight journey.

References

Chapter 1

Johnson, S. (2010). *Where Good Ideas Come From.* New York, NY: Riverhead Books.

Popova, M. (n.d.). Mission. Retrieved from https://www.brainpickings.org/mission/rg/mission.

Barlow, A. (1879). *The History and Principles of Weaving – By Hand and by Power.* London: Samson Low, Marston, Searle & Rivington.

McLeish, T. (2019). *The Poetry and Music of Science.* Oxford, UK: Oxford University Press.

Chapter 2

James, W. (1925). *Talks to Teachers on Psychology: And to students on some of life's ideals.* New York, NY: Henry Holt and Company.

Rooper, T.G. (1892). *A Pot of Green Feathers: A study in apperception.* New York, NY: E. L. Kellogg & Co.

Questlove. (2018). *Creative Quest.* New York, NY: HarperCollins.

Wurman, R.S. (1989). *Information Anxiety.* New York, NY: DoubleDay.

Chapter 3

Ditto, P.H., Clark C.J., Liu, B.S., Wojcik, S.P., Chen, E.E., Grady, R.H., Celniker, J.B., & Zinger, J.F. (2018). At Least Bias Is Bipartisan: A Meta-Analytic Comparison of Partisan Bias in Liberals and Conservatives. *Perspectives on Psychological Science, 14*(2), 273-291. doi: 10.1177/1745691617746796.

Hippocrates. (1931). *Hippocrates Volume IV: Nature of Man. Regimen in Health. Humours. Aphorisms. Regimen 1-3. Dreams. Heracleitus: On the Universe.* (W.H.S. Jones, Trans.). Cambridge, MA: Harvard University Press.

Lobotomy. (n.d.). Retrieved December 27, 2019 from https://en.wikipedia.org/wiki/Lobotomy.

Chapter 4

Shermer, M. (2012). *The Believing Brain: From Ghosts and Gods to Politics and Conspiracies---How We Construct Beliefs and Reinforce Them as Truths.* New York, NY: St. Martin's Griffin.

Chater, N. (2018). *The Mind is Flat: The Remarkable Shallowness of the Improvising Brain.* New Haven, CT: Yale University Press.

Bruner, J.S., & Postman, L. (1949). On the Perception of Incongruity: A Paradigm. *Journal of Personality, 18,* 206–223. doi.org/10.1111/j.1467-6494.1949.tb01241.x.

Gaissmaier, W., Wilke, A., Scheibehenne, B., McCanney, P., & Barrett H.C. (2016). Betting on Illusory Patterns: Probability Matching in Habitual Gamblers. *Journal of Gambling Studies, 32*(1),143-56. doi: 10.1007/s10899-015-9539-9.

Nasar, S. (1994, November 13). The Lost Years of a Nobel Laureate. *New York Times.* Section 3, p 1.

Nisbett, R.E., & Wilson, T.D. (1977). Telling more than we can know: Verbal reports on mental processes. *Psychological Review, 84*(3), 231–259. doi.org/10.1037/0033-295X.84.3.231

The Choice Blindness Lab has a useful website which contains links to many of their studies. You can access it here: www.lucs.lu.se/choice-blindness-group.

Inc. Video. (n.d.). What you see is not all there is. Retrieved from https://www.inc.com/daniel-kahneman/idea-lab-what-you-see-not-all-there-is.html.

Winerman L. (2012). 'A machine for jumping to conclusions': An interview with Daniel Kahenman, *Monitor, 43*(2), 24.

Spurious Correlations. (n.d.). Retrieved from http://tylervigen.com./spurious-correlations.

Chapter 5

Wasserstein, R.L., & Lazar, L.A. (2016). The ASA Statement on p-Values: Context, Process, and Purpose, The American Statistician, 70(2), 129-133. doi: 10.1080/00031305.2016.1154108.

Nuzzo, R. (2014). Scientific method: Statistical errors. Nature, 506(7487), 150-152. doi: 10.1038/506150a.

Camerer, C.F., Dreber, A., Holzmeister, F., Ho, T., Huber, J., Johannesson, M., Kirchler, M., Nave, G., Nosek, B.A., Pfeiffer, T., Altmejd, A., Buttrick, N., Chan, T., Chen, Y., Forsell, E., Gampa, A., Heikensten, E., Hummer, L., Imai, T., Isaksson, S., Manfredi, D., Rose, J., Wagenmakers, E., & Wu, H. (2018). Evaluating the replicability of social science experiments in *Nature* and *Science* between 2010 and 2015. *Nature Human Behaviour, 2,* 637-644.

Wansink, B. (2011). *Mindless Eating: Why We Eat More Than We Think.* Carlsbad, CA: Hay House.

Wansink, B. (2014). *Slim by Design: Mindless Eating for Everyday Life*. New York, NY: William Morrow.

Amrhein, V., Greenland, S., & McShane, B. (2019). Nature, 567(7748), 305-307. doi: 10.1038/d41586-019-00857-9.
Fisher, R.A. (1937). *The Design of Experiments*. (2nd ed.). New York, NY: Hafner.

Gigerenzer, G. (2018). Statistical Rituals: The Replication Delusion and How We Got There. *Advances in Methods and Practices in Psychological Science*, 1(2), 198–218. doi: 10.1177/2515245918771329.

Chapter 6

Horowitz, A. (2010). *Inside of a Dog: What Dogs See, Smell and Know*. New York, NY: Scribner.

Novella, S. with Novella, B., Santa Maria, C., Novella, J., & Bernstein, E. (2018). *The Skeptics' Guide to the Universe: How to Know What's Really Real in a World Increasingly Full of Fake*. New York, NY: Grand Central.

Dyèvre, A. (2015). Intelligence, the human factor and cognitive biases. Retrieved from https://ceis.eu/fr/strategic-note-intelligence-the-human-factor-and-cognitive-biases/.

Walton, T. (2010). *Challenges in Intelligence Analysis: Lessons from 1300 BCE to the Present*. Cambridge, UK: Cambridge University Press.

Croskerry, P. (2013). From Mindless to Mindful Practice—Cognitive Bias and Clinical Decision Making, *New England Journal of Medicine*, 368, 2445-2448. doi: 10.1056/NEJMp1303712.

Rossmo, K., & Pollock, J. (2019). Confirmation Bias and Other Systemic Causes of Wrongful Convictions: A Sentinel Events Perspective. *Northeastern University Law Review, 11*(2), 790-835. doi.org/10.2139/ssrn.3413922.

Chapter 7

Findley, K.A., & Scott, M.S. (2006). The Multiple Dimensions of Tunnel Vision in Criminal Cases. *Univ. of Wisconsin Legal Studies Research Paper No. 1023*. Retrieved from https://ssrn.com/ abstract=911240.

Wilson, P.J. (2003). *Wrongful Convictions: Lessons learned from the Sophonow Public Inquiry*. Winnipeg, MB: Canadian Police College.

Chapter 8

Johnston, R. (2005). *Analytic Culture in the U.S. Intelligence Community: An Ethnographic Study*. Washington, DC: Center for the Study of Intelligence, Central Intelligence Agency.

Kent, S. (1955). The Need for an Intelligence Literature. *Studies in Intelligence*, 4. Retrieved from https://www.cia.gov/library/center-for-the-study-of-intelligence/csi-publications/books-and-monographs/sherman-kent-and-the-board-of-national-estimates-collected-essays/2need.html.

Kent, S. (1941). *Writing History*. New York, NY: F.S. Crofts and Company.

Ford, H. P. (1980). A Tribute to Sherman Kent. *Studies in Intelligence*, 4. Retrieved from https://www.cia.gov/library/center-for-the-study-of-intelligence/csi-publications/books-and-monographs/sherman-kent-and-the-board-of-national-estimates-collected-essays/1tribute.html.

Winks, R.W. (1987). *Cloak & Gown: Scholars in the Secret War, 1939–1961* (2nd ed.). New Haven, CT: Yale University Press.

Davis, J. (2005). Sherman Kent and the Profession of Intelligence Analysis. *The Sherman Kent Center for Intelligence Analysis Occasional Papers, 1*(5). Retrieved from https://www.cia.gov/library/kent-center-occasional-papers/vol1no5.html.

Kent, S. (1949). *Strategic Intelligence for American World Policy*. Princeton, NJ: Princeton University Press.

Scoblic, J.P. (2018). Beacon and Warning: Sherman Kent, Scientific Hubris, and the CIA's Office of National Estimates. *Texas National Security Review, 1*(4), 98-129.

Heuer, R. J. Jr. (1999). *Psychology of Intelligence Analysis*. Washington, DC: Center for the Study of Intelligence, Central Intelligence Agency.

Heuer, R. J. Jr. (2009). The Evolution of Structured Analytic Techniques. *Presentation to the National Academy of Science, National Research Council Committee on Behavioral and Social Science Research to Improve Intelligence Analysis for National Security*. Retrieved from https://www.e-education.psu.edu/ geog885/sites/www.e-education.psu.edu.geog885/files/file/ Evolution_SAT_Heuer.pdf.

Chapter 9

Mandel, D.R., & Barnes, A. (2014). Accuracy of strategic intelligence forecasts. *Proceedings of the National Academy of Sciences, 111*(30), 10984-10989. doi: 10.1073/pnas.1406138111.

Dhami, M.K., Belton, I. & Mandel, D.R., (2019). The "analysis of competing hypotheses" in intelligence analysis. *Applied Cognitive Psychology, 33*(6), 1080-1090. doi:10.1002/acp.3550.

Chang, W., Berdinni, E., Mandel, D.R., & Tetlock, P. E. (2017). Restructuring structured analytic techniques in intelligence. *Intelligence and National Security, 33*(3), 337-356. doi: 10.1080/02684527.2017.1400230.

Mandel, D.R., & Tetlock, P.E. (2018). Correcting Judgment Correctives in National Security Intelligence. *Frontiers in Psychology, 9*, Article 2640. doi: 10.3389/fpsyg.2018.02640.

Mellers, B., Stone, E., Atanasov, P., Rohrbaugh, N., Metz, S.E., Ungar, L., Bishop, M. M., Horowitz, M., Merkle, E. & Tetlock, P. (2015). The Psychology of Intelligence Analysis: Drivers of Prediction Accuracy in

World Politics. *Journal of Experimental Psychology: Applied 21*(1), 1–14. doi: 10.1037/xap0000040

Building Business Impact Handbook. (2019). Global Research Business Network. Retrieved from https://grbn.org/impact/handbook/.

Chapter 10

James, T. (2017, December). Can Cops Unlearn Their Unconscious Biases? *The Atlantic.* Retrieved from https://www.theatlantic.com/politics/archive/ 2017/12/implicit-bias-training-salt-lake/548996/

Davis, J. (2008). Why Bad Things Happen to Good Analysts. In R. Z. George and J. B. Bruce (Eds.), *Analyzing Intelligence: Origins, Obstacles, and Innovations* (pp. 121-134). Washington, DC: Georgetown University Press.

Graber, M.L., Kissam, S., Payne, V.L., Meyer, A.N.D., Sorensen, A., Lenfestey, N., Tant, E., Henriksen, K., LaBresh, K., & Singh, H. (2012). Cognitive interventions to reduce diagnostic error: A narrative review. *BMJ Quality & Safety 21*(7), 535-57. doi: 10.1136/bmjqs-2011-000149

Saposnik, G., Redelmeier, D.A., Ruff, C.C., & Tobler, P.N. (2016). Cognitive biases associated with medical decisions: A systematic review. *BMC Medical Informatics and Decision Making, 16*, Article number: 138.

Burke, A.S. (2007). Neutralizing Cognitive Bias: An Invitation to Prosecutors *N.Y.U. Journal of Law & Liberty 2*(3), 512-530.

O'Sullivan, E.D., & Schofield, S.J. (2018). Cognitive Bias in Clinical Medicine. *Journal of the Royal College of Physicians of Edinburgh, 48*(3), 225-232. doi: 10.4997/JRCPE.2018.306.

Chapter 11

Levey, M. (1967). *Medical ethics of medieval Islam: With special reference to al-Ruhāwī's Practical ethics of the physician (Transactions of the American Philosophical Society)*. Philadelphia, PA: American Philosophical Society.

National Research Council. (2011). *Intelligence Analysis for Tomorrow: Advances from the Behavioral and Social Sciences*. Washington, DC: The National Academies Press.

Chapter 12

Russell, B. (1922). *Free Thought and Official Propaganda*. London, UK: Watts & Co.

Rilke, R. M. (1993) *Letters to a Young Poet* (H. Norton, Trans.). New York, NY: W.W. Norton & Co. (Original work published 1929).

Sagan, S., & Druyan, A. (1995). *The Demon-Haunted World: Science as a Candle in the Dark*. New York, NY: Random House.

Tetlock, P.E., & Gardner, D. (2015). *Superforecasting: The Art and Science of Prediction*. New York, NY: Broadway Books.

CBC News. (2012). Woman's heart concerns dismissed, says grieving husband. Retrieved from https://www.cbc.ca/news/canada/manitoba/woman-s-heart-concerns-dismissed-says-grieving-husband-1.1260646

Doyle, A.C. (1894). *The Memoirs of Sherlock Holmes*. London, UK: George Newnes.

Dobelli, R. (2014). *The Art of Thinking Clearly* (N. Griffin, Trans.). New York, NY: HarperCollins.

Wald, A. (1943). *A Reprint of "A Method of Estimating Plane Vulnerability Based on Damage of Survivors."* Alexandrea, VA: Center for Naval Analyses.

Chapter 13

Gawande, A. (2009). *The Checklist Manifesto: How to Get Things Right*. New York, NY: Picador.

Chapter 14

Johnson, D., Johnson, J., & Hilborn, J. (1992). *Electric Circuit Analysis* Englewood Cliffs, NJ: Prentice Hall.
Woodworth, R. S. (1938). *Experimental Psychology*. New York, NY: H. Holt and Company.

Poincaré, H. (1914). *Science and Method* (F. Maitland, Trans.). London, UK: Thomas Nelson and Sons. (Original published 1913).

Wallas, G. (1926). *The Art of Thought*. New York, NY: Harcourt, Brace & Company.
Young, J. W. (1940). *A Technique for Producing Ideas*. Detroit, MI: Crain Communications.

Beadle, P. (2011). *Dancing about Architecture: A Little Book of Creativity*. Bethel, CT: Crown House.

Chapter 15

Darwin, C. (1839/2009) *Charles Darwin's notebooks from the voyage of the Beagle*. G. Chancellor & J. van Wyhe, with the assistance of K. Rookmaaker (Eds.). Cambridge, UK: Cambridge University Press.

Kounios, J., Beeman, M., with Kounios, Y. S. (2015). *The Eureka Factor: Aha Moments, Creative Insight, and the Brain*. New York, NY: Random House.

Beveridge, W.I.B. (1950) *The Art of Scientific Investigation*. New York, NY: W.W. Norton & Company.

Chapter 16

Anonymous. (1722). *The Travels and Adventures of Three Princes of Serendip.* London, UK: Will. Chetwode.

Walpole, H. (1748/1958). *The Yale Edition of Horace Walpole's Correspondence, Volume 17.* W. S. Lewis (Ed.). New Haven, CT: Yale University Press.

Merton, R.K., & Barber, E. (2004). *The Travels and Adventures of Serendipity: A Study in Sociological Semantics and the Sociology of Science.* Princeton, NJ: Princeton University Press.

Einstein, A., & Infeld, L. (1938). *The Evolution of Physics.* Cambridge, UK: Cambridge University Press.

Dunbar, K. (1999). How Scientists Build Models: InVivo Science as a Window on the Scientific Mind. In L. Magnani, N.J. Nersessian, & P. Thagard (Eds.) *Model-based Reasoning in Scientific Discovery* (pp. 89-98). New York, NY: Plenum.

Surowiecki, J. (2004) *The Wisdom of Crowds: Why the Many Are Smarter Than the Few and How Collective Wisdom Shapes Business, Economies, Societies and Nations.* New York, NY: Doubleday.

Chi, M.T.H., Feltovich, P.J., & Glaser, R. (1981). Categorization and Representation of Physics Problems by Experts and Novices. *Cognitive Science: A Multidisciplinary Journal 5*(2), 121-152. doi: 10.1207/s15516709cog0502_2.

Rottman, B.M., Genter, D., & Goldwater, M.B. (2012). Causal Systems Categories: Differences in Novice and Expert Categorization of Causal Phenomena. *Cognitive Science—A Multidisciplinary Journal 36*(5), 919-932. doi: 10.1111/j.1551-6709.2012.01253.x.

Darwin, C. (1958). *The Autobiography of Charles Darwin 1809-1882. With the original omissions restored. Edited and with appendix and notes by his granddaughter Nora Barlow.* F. Darwin & N. Barlow (Eds.). London, UK: Collins.

Chapter 17

John Cleese speaking at the 2009 Creativity World Forum in Germany. Retrieved from www.openculture.com/2010/09/ john_cleese_on_the_origin_of_creativity.

Tufte, E. (1983). *The Visual Display of Quantitative Information*. Cheshire, CT: Graphics.

Oppezzo, M., & Schwartz, D.L. (2014). Give Your Ideas Some Legs: The Positive Effect of Walking on Creative Thinking. *Journal of Experimental Psychology: Learning, Memory, and Cognition, 40*(4), 1142–1152. doi: 10.1037/a0036577.

Beck, H. (2019). *Scatterbrain: How the Mind's Mistakes Make Humans Creative, Innovative and Successful* (B.L. Crook, Trans.). Vancouver, BC: Greystone.

Pillay, S. (2017). Your Brain Can Only Take So Much Focus. *Harvard Business Review*, Retrieved from https://hbr.org/2017/05/ your-brain-can-only-take-so-much-focus.

Pillay, S. (2017). *Tinker, Dabble, Doodle, Try: Unlock the Power of the Unfocused Mind*. New York, NY: Ballantine.

Swett, O. (1901). *How They Succeeded: Life Stories of Successful Men Told by Themselves*. Boston, MA: Lothrop.

Cai D.J., Mednick, S.A., Harrison, E.M., Kanady J.C., & Mednick, S.C. (2009). REM, not incubation, improves creativity by priming associative networks. *Proceedings of the National Academy of Sciences 106*(25), 10130-10134. doi: 10.1073/pnas.0900271106

Stickgold, R. (2019). Creativity of the Dream and Sleep State. In *Secrets of Creativity: What Neuroscience, the Arts, and Our Minds Reveal*. S. Nalbantian & P.M. Matthews (Eds.). Oxford, UK: Oxford University Press.

Verleger, R., Rose, M., Wagner, U., Yordanova, J., & Kolev, V. (2013). Insights into sleep's role for insight: Studies with the number reduction task. *Advances in Cognitive Psychology 9*(4), 160–172. doi: 10.2478/v10053-008-0143-8.

Lewis, P.A., Knoblich, G., & Poe, G. (2018). How Memory Replay in Sleep Boosts Creative Problem-Solving. *Trends in Cognitive Sciences 22*(6), 491-503. doi: 10.1016/j.tics.2018.03.009.

Abraham, A. (2018). *The Neuroscience of Creativity.* Cambridge, UK: Cambridge University Press.

Klein, G. (2013). *Seeing What Others Don't: The Remarkable Ways We Gain Insights.* New York, NY: Public Affairs.

Chapter 18

Grierson, B. (2015, March). Eureka! *Psychology Today.* Retrieved from https://www.psychologytoday.com/us/articles/201503/eureka.

Metcalfe, J., & Wiebe, D. (1987). Intuition in insight and noninsight problem solving. *Memory & Cognition 15*, 238–246. doi:10.3758/BF03197722.

Topolinski, S., & Reber, R. (2010). Gaining Insight Into the 'Aha' Experience. *Current Directions in Psychological Science 19*(6), 402-405. doi: 10.1177/0963721410388803.

Keller, E.F. (1983). *A Feeling for the Organism, 10th Anniversary Edition: The Life and Work of Barbara McClintock.* New York, NY: Henry Holt and Company.

Vazquez J., & Baghdoyan, H.A. (2001). Basal forebrain acetylcholine release during REM sleep is significantly greater than during waking. *American Journal of Physiology Regulatory, Integrative and Comparative Physiology 280*(2), R598-R601. doi:10.1152/ajpregu.2001.280.2.R598

Otto Loewi. (n.d.). Retrieved from https://en.wikipedia.org/wiki/Otto_Loewi.

Lachaîne, A., Lowe, A., Forbes, G., Hurley, M., & Grenville, A. (1998). Retrieved from https://soundcloud.com/5th_dimentia/i-shouda-wrote-it-down.

Graves, R.P. (1885). *The Life of Sir William Robert Hamilton, Royal Astronomer of Ireland Volume II*. Dublin, IE: Hodge, Figgis and Co.

Danek, A. H., & Wiley, J. (2017). What about false insights? Deconstructing the aha! Experience along its multiple dimensions for correct and incorrect solutions separately. *Frontiers in Psychology, 7*, Article 2077. doi: 10.3389/fpsyg.2016.02077

Chapter 19

Burton, R. (2008). *On Being Certain: Believing You Are Right Even When You are Not*. New York, NY: St. Martin's Griffin.

Haldane, J.B.S. (1963). The Truth About Death. *Journal of Genetics, 58*(3), 452–454.

Khun, T.S. (1962). *The Structure of Scientific Revolutions*. Chicago, IL: University of Chicago Press.

Mueller, J., Melwani, S., & Goncalo, J.A. (2011). The Bias Against Creativity: Why People Desire But Reject Creative Ideas. *Psychological Science, 23*(1), 13-17. doi: 10.1177/0956797611421018.

Nuland, S. B. (2004). *The Doctors' Plague: Germs, Childbed Fever, and the Strange Story of Ignác Semmelweis*. New York, NY: W. W. Norton & Company.

Semmelweis, I. (1983). *The Etiology, Concept, and Prophylaxis of Childbed Fever*. (K. Codell Carter, Trans.). Madison, WI: University of Wisconsin Press.

Chapter 20

Popova, M. (2014). Wisdom in the Age of Information and the Importance of Storytelling in Making Sense of the World: An Animated Essay. Retrieved from https://www.brainpickings.org/2014/09/09/wisdom-in-the-age-of-information/

Effective Communication. (n.d). *Nature*. Retrieved from
https://www.nature.com/scitable/topicpage/effective-communication-
13950970/

United States Army. (2013). *Army Regulation 25-50. Preparing and Managing
Correspondence.* Washington, DC: Department of the Army.

Sontag, S. (2007). *At the Same Time: Essays and Speeches.* P. Dilonardo &
A. Jump (Eds.). New York, NY: Farrar, Straus and Giroux.
Kleon, A. (2012). *Steal Like An Artist.* New York, NY: Workman.

Orwell, G. (1946). Politics and the English Language. *Horizon: A Review
of Literature and Art, 13*(76), 252–265.

Forer, B. (1949). The fallacy of personal validation: A classroom
demonstration of gullibility. *Journal of Abnormal and Social Psychology, 44*(1),
118–123.

Kent, S. (1964). Words of Estimative Probability. *Studies in Intelligence, 4.*

Barnes, A. (2016). Making Intelligence Analysis More Intelligent: Using
Numeric Probabilities, *Intelligence and National Security, 31*(3), 327-344.
doi: 10.1080/02684527.2014.994955.

Acknowledgements

Grenville, A. (2018). *The Insights Revolution: Questioning Everything.*
Toronto, ON: Maru/Matchbox.

Grenville, B., Augaitis, D., & Rebick, S. (Eds.). (2016). *MashUp: The Birth
of Modern Culture.* Vancouver, BC: Black Dog Publishing, Vancouver Art
Gallery.